My Brother

LARRY

The Stooge In The Middle

by Morris "Moe" Feinberg
with
G.P Skratz

Edited and Researched
by Bob Davis

with additional research by:

Mark Gilman   Jeff Lenburg
Tom Prosek   Greg Lenburg
         Steve Cox

Foreword by Steve Allen
Preface by Steve Cox
Illustrations by Drew Friedman

Graphic Design by Richard Zybert

Published by Last Gasp of San Francisco

Dedicated to my dear wife Dinah, who put up with the incessant clatter of my typewriter, day and night, without complaint while I was writing this book, and to the memory of my beloved brother Larry, without whom there would be no book to write.

ACKNOWLEDGEMENTS

Steve Allen
Dale Ashmus
Bill Ballantine
Edward Bernds
Dawn Berry
Lester Borden
Oscar Brand
Powell Burns
Kate Chervenak
Charles Compagnucci
Florence Davis
Jordan Davis
George DiCaprio
Alissa Elkin
Paul Fericano
Jerome Field
Larry Fine Archive of New York
Jeff Forester
Paul "Mousie" Garner
Alan Hale
Van Joyce
Linda Lemon
The Raymond Mander & Joe Mitchenson Theater Collection
Ann Miller
Bob Mogill
Brian Mulhern
Madeline Muller

Mark Newgarden
Joe Ohliger III
Pat's Steaks
Carol Schwamberger
Tom Shafer
Theodore Shank
Emil Sitka
Doug Skinner
Randy Skretvedt
Sally Starr
Stoll Moss Theaters, Ltd
Dave Stuckey
Dorothy Swerdlove.
Evelyn Tecotzky
Joe Wallison
Don Williams
Johnny Williams
Bill Winberg
Mark Yurkin

And special thanks to Andy Levinson

Graphic Design: Richard Zybert
Layout/Design: Howard Munson
Layout: James Stark
Typesetting: Jennifer Poole

Published and distributed by:

Last Gasp of San Francisco
777 Florida Street
San Francisco, CA 94110
www.lastgasp.com

For Stooges information:

Three Stooges Fan Club
P.O. Box 747
Gwynedd Valley, PA 19437
GaryStooge@aol.com

ISBN: 0-86719-324-7 hardcover
0-86719-308-5 softcover

The following photographs are used with permission:

©1984, 2000 Columbia Pictures, Inc.
Pages 16, 114, 150, 160 (upper), 164, 175 (lower).

Billy Rose Theater Collection, The New York Public Library at Lincoln Center.
Pages: 56, 60, 71, 139

Selections from *Visions of Cody* by Jack Kerouac are reprinted by permission of
The Sterling Lord Agency, Inc. Copyright ©1972 by Jack Kerouac

Comic lyrics to "Humoresque" by Oscar Brand are used with permission of the author.

Printed in Hong Kong

TABLE OF CONTENTS

Larry Fine.
(from the collection of Joe Wallison)

LARRY: THE STOOGE IN THE MIDDLE 〰〰〰
by Steve Allen

Theologians have argued for centuries as to whether the commandments referred to in the Old Testament were actually 10 in number. Strictly speaking, they were not. It will therefore perhaps not come as too great a shock to most readers to learn that there were more than four Marx Brothers, and a great many more than three Stooges. Indeed, the only justification for calling them the Three Stooges at all was that only three of them appeared at any given time.

It is fascinating, and entirely fitting, that in recent years the Stooges are finally being granted a degree of critical respect and nostalgic appreciation that was largely denied them in their prime. Their fate in this regard has been rather like that of Abbott & Costello, in that during the days when they were doing most of their pictures, critics paid them very little attention. What has occasioned the turn-about? Probably nothing more complicated than that the millions of ten-to-15-year-olds who considered both the Stooges and Bud and Lou every bit as funny as the Marx Brothers or Laurel & Hardy, have now grown up, and find themselves fondly remembering their childhood favorites. This somewhat begs the original question: were the Three Stooges as clever, as innately funny, as the acknowledged giants of knockabout film comedy? Well, by certain standards of judgement, no, not quite. But this is certainly not a matter calling for an either-or judgement. As regards performing in certain kinds of wild, unrealistic sketches, I don't consider myself as funny as Sid Caesar, but that does not mean I am prepared to get out of show business.

It has always been difficult to make comparative judgements in the arts, simply because there are no easily measurable factors. If one man runs the hundred-meter dash half a second faster than another, and does so consistently, then he is obviously the better runner. As regards comedy, there has never been such a thing as a universally popular comedian, from which it seems reasonable to conclude that there never will be. The only American performer who ever came close was Will Rogers, and I would guess that there were a few film fans in the 1930s who did not participate in the otherwise general adulation accorded the witty cowboy philosopher. The reader may be surprised to learn, incidentally, that factors other than the simple element of funniness determine the overall popularity of a comedian. Almost everyone — including, very probably, Bob Hope himself — would judge Bob is less funny than, say, Jonathan Winters. But Hope is certainly the more popular. So the generation, as I say, that held the Three Stooges in high esteem, having come of voting age and then some, is now determined to give the Stooges their rightful place in the Pantheon of important comedians.

To return to the factor of comparisons, the Stooges are superior to not only most traditional comedians but to almost all present practitioners of the trade, so far as slapstick comedy is concerned. They did their share of word-play jokes, too, though not nearly as much as did the Marx Brothers. But they rank close to some of the silent screen greats (Chaplin, Laurel and Hardy, Buster Keaton, Harold Lloyd) when it comes to bumping-into-each-other, falling-down, pie-in-the-face comedy.

The Stooges were masters of that particular game. Considering that they inflicted, and suffered, an incredible amount of physical punishment, it is interesting that no character in their films was ever killed or even seriously injured. This was true of both silent and talkies slapstick in general, as it was of animated cartoons. The physical mayhem committed in cartoons obviously goes far beyond what could occur in either the world of reality or regular motion pictures. Assorted cartoon dogs, cats, coyotes, ducks and other animals run into brick walls at full speed, fall off cliffs, bounce unsuspectingly into alligators' mouths, etc. and although they are often visibly the worse for wear after such surprises, they are still on their feet and running about. Just so it has been with the Stooges. No matter how many times their eyeballs are poked with forked fingers, no matter how many times their faces are soundly slapped, how many times they are tripped and sent sprawling, how many times they fall out of windows, they never seem to suffer the logical consequences.

Morris Feinberg has an angle of vision about the Stooges not granted to any other student of their art for the reason that he was of the family, being the younger brother of Larry Fine. His report provides interesting insights into the long-gone world of vaudeville.

Larry, Curly-Joe, and Moe (kneeling) on The Steve Allen Show, April 5, 1959. Standing behind the Stooges are Connie Russell, Louis Nye, Steve Allen, Tom Posten, David Allen and Don Knotts (used by permission of Steve Allen)

A FAN LOOKS AT LARRY
by Steve Cox

When I was asked to write a preface for a book about Larry, I thought, "WOW!" This honor would flatter statesmen, inspire poets, and make innumerable Stooge fans green with envy!

Serving the Three Stooges Club, Inc. as Moe Feinberg's Vice-President, I have had the great pleasure of getting to know many "Stooge notables" and helping on books, TV shows, and other projects.

Actor Alan Hale, Jr., of *Gilligan's Island* fame, recently told me some great stories about his friendship with Larry.

Both Larry and Alan were members of the "Hollywood Hackers," a golf club. "Larry was marvelously helpless," Hale explained. "He would even carry his daughter's golf clubs and use them instead of his own, because his were too heavy."

"You could describe our relationship as 'lost in the supermarket'," Hale laughed. Then he cupped his hands and yelled, "Alan, where are you?" just like Larry would after getting lost in the toilet paper section of Hughes Market in LA.

"Larry was very funny in his own lovable way. I was quite fond of him, and I would call him just a wonderful little guy with a humor all his own," Hale concluded.

Larry was a little guy. In fact he barely stood 5'4" and weighed 145 lb. Most people don't realize how short the Stooges were.

The films present Larry as a third banana. But he played himself, a happy-go-lucky fellow who would rather have fun than work. I feel he was always game, willing to be swept up into all kinds of projects and pleasures that promised a chance for small adventures and momentary flushes of excitement.

Larry loved to spend money. He once said his two favorite hobbies were sleeping and buying big cars. He loved to go to the races. Sometimes he could be found at the local track instead of rehearsal.

When Larry would screw up on the set of a Stooges' film, Moe Howard would really let him have it. In front of the whole crew, he'd call Larry a stupid this or a stupid that. In fact, years later, when Larry resided in the Motion Picture Actors' rest home, Moe would drop by every other week to harass him for old time's sake.

Larry has been tagged with a lot of complimentary titles, too, and I must add one more: family doctor. Larry and the Stooges have made more house calls than any physician on record. They pop into my house and brighten my day at times when I most need it. He, Moe, and the rest seem to lighten my load and lift my burdens.

So, thank you, Larry, for the wonderful hours of pleasure and happiness you have supplied to millions of Stooge fans.

SHOWTIME 〜〜〜〜〜〜〜〜〜〜〜〜〜

Marty Bohn and Nancy Lee, tireless troopers of the small club circuit, were headlining at The Dude Ranch, a nightclub in Atlantic City. Marty spotted me in the audience and signalled the drummer: a quick roll on the snare.

"I don't usually tell this story, Ladies and Gentlemen." He was confiding in the crowd, making everyone feel at home. "But many years ago, I was in an act with Larry Fine, one of The Three Stooges. Now in the audience tonight, I see Larry's brother, Moe Fine, a good friend and fellow performer. Moe, would you stand up and take a bow."

The spotlight went sailing from Marty's outstretched hand to the table where my wife, Dinah, and I were sitting. I stood in the applause, nodded, and took my bow.

A few minutes later, I felt a tap on my shoulder. It was a young lady, waving a pencil and a scrap of paper like a tiny flag on the Fourth of July.

"May I have your autograph?"

"What do you want with my autograph?" I chuckled. "I'm no celebrity."

"You can't fool me with that 'brother' stuff," she smiled, looking me over. "You're Larry, all right."

Never argue with a fan. You never win. I know: I'm a fan, myself.

"With warm regards," I wrote. "Larry 'Stooge' Fine."

INTRODUCTIONS 〜〜〜〜〜〜〜〜〜〜〜〜〜

"Meet my friend, Moe Feinberg."

That might have been one way to introduce me to someone. Here was the more common way:

"Take a good look at this guy. Who does he remind you of? Oh, come on. Ever hear of The Three Stooges? Take a guess. One of them is his brother. See a resemblance?

They'd muss up my hair. They'd pretend to slap me around. They'd grab my hand and poke my fingers at their eyes.

Larry used to get a big kick out of introducing me to his show business friends as his "little brother." And I was, indeed, two years younger than he. But I was about four or

Morris "Moe" Feinberg & Dinah Feinberg, 1980.

five inches taller. When I was ten, I had my tonsils and adenoids taken out, and that somehow triggered an extra growing spurt. Larry stopped growing at five feet four. Sometimes, he'd even wear elevator shoes to make himself look taller. So the term, "little brother," became a bit of a joke.

"Meet my little brother," he'd say, then double up with laughter.

THE CLEARING OF THE THROAT

My brother, the movie star: I used to look at the marquees, his face on the posters, and shake my head. He actually did it. There he was, with his partners, in movies with Clark Gable, Joan Crawford, Fred Astaire, Spencer Tracy — a "Who's Who" of cinema.

He spiced my life with a happy hint of celebrity. I was in the window-dressing business, and I was good at it. But I wasn't immune to the magic of stage and screen. I enjoyed crossing paths with people like Edward G. Robinson during my off-hours. Or Dean Martin. Or Shecky Greene. Or George Burns. Hey, the list goes on. Stick around: I'll introduce you.

But he wasn't just a movie star. He wasn't surrounded by swooning romantics hoping for a date or a lock of his electric hair. Nor was he accosted by film scholars seeking the hidden meanings in his latest work. He was a clown, the stooge in the middle of the three most incorrigible clowns in the business. No apologies to the intellectuals; no goal higher than the belly laugh. And the audience has been in hysterics for more than half a century.

But he wasn't just a clown: he was a family man. He didn't write much, but he called on the phone from almost anywhere. He never missed at birthdays and holidays. And I wouldn't be surprised if the phone company had a special "Larry Fine" award for the guy who racked up the highest bill during the Hanukah/Christmas season.

He touched my life deeply on all these levels. And here is our family album, snapshots in words.

On with the show!

DESTINY ～～～～～～～～～～～～～～～～～～

Everyone begins at the beginning. Want a beginning? Here's before the beginning:

It was the 1890's, in Philadelphia. Mother was a teenager. And she was going off with some girlfriends to have her fortune read by a gypsy.

In those days, gypsies used to live in fairly rundown housing. Four or five families would share a rented storefront in the winter. And in the summertime, they'd live in wagons, in the open air. In either event, it was considered "daring" for young ladies, not of their clan, to visit them.

They met a friendly old woman, delighted to see them. She took Mother aside: "You will marry," she whispered. "And have a son known all over the world."

Perhaps she said that to all the girls. But you and I know what she couldn't know, not for sure: she was right.

9

The Old Country was Russia. The family name: Frienchi-cov (pronounced: free-n-chick). The Frienchicovs were Jew-ish, and this was the family goal: to get the hell out of Russia.

Russia had always been anti-Semitic, and the Jews had always endured. But history took a savage turn in 1881. Czar Alexander II was assassinated, and rumor had it that his killer was Jewish. The rumor, it turned out, was wrong. But you couldn't tell that to the blood-thirsty mobs that sprang up in hundreds of cities, eager for revenge. The government did little to stop them. Some officials even joined them. And thus was the birth of the pogroms, the mob massacres that were to plague Russia for decades and then spread west through Eastern Europe to Germany.

Dad was Joseph Frienchicov, a watchmaker earning mon-ey to emigrate. He was well on his way to freedom when the bitter summons came: he was drafted.

If the civilian world was forbidding, the army was impos-sible. It was a snakepit of anti-Semitism. But Dad came up with a scheme to make army life liveable. He was a fairly good horn player, and he decided to try out for the Army Band. Think of it: a Jew in the Czar's Army Band! He'd be invulnerable.

He got the part, and he really got a kick out of it. Show busi-ness seems to run in the family.

But here was Dad's surprise: his sergeant's cousin had al-ready tried out for the part and had failed the audition.

His sergeant hated him.

One day, Dad fell asleep on sentry duty, and his sergeant spotted him. He crept up to Dad and took his gun. This was deep trouble: sleeping on watch was one thing, but losing your gun on watch meant a trip to the firing squad. Fortun-ately, Dad woke up just as the sergeant was sneaking away. He sprang up and whacked him one. He grabbed his gun and was back at his post.

The sergeant couldn't report him. Army policy was simply to awaken sleeping sentries, not steal their guns. So he was home free — for awhile. Who knew for how long?

Dad didn't chance it. He vanished: absent without leave.

He fled to England and became Joseph Frank, a watchmaker again. His brother Nathan was already in America and had adopted the name, Feinberg. And as soon as he could, Dad himself booked passage on a ratty old steamer jammed beyond reason with hundreds and hundreds of his compatriots. Everyone was seasick. You couldn't smell the ocean for all the sweat and vomit. And at night, they recalled the old Yiddish proverb: "Sleep fast, we need the pillows."

But they dreamed the great dream: they were headed for the Statue of Liberty.

BABY PICTURES ~~~~~~~~~~~~~~~~~~~~~~~

At the turn of the century, in the exotic new land of South Philadelphia, Joseph Feinberg and Fannie Lieberman met and fell in love. Dad was in a daze. He would ride his bicycle to the Liebermans' house, spend a few hours with Mother, then walk home, forgetting all about his bike.

Dad wasn't in bad shape financially. The jeweler's art spans the seas with relative ease. And Dad had been quick to set up a successful watch repair and jewelry store. He could afford to support the love of his life and begin a family.

So Mother became Mrs. Fannie Feinberg and moved into the second floor apartment above Dad's storefront at 606 S. Third Street.

The family began arriving on October 5, 1902. It was then that, in their tiny bedroom, Mother presented Dad with their first child, a son. He was named Louis. We called him Louie. You know him as Larry.

Two years later, on September 5, 1904, I came along. "Yuck, he's ugly," remarked my dear brother Larry. "Throw him out the window." Just jealous, I guess.

Two more years swept by, and it was December 21, 1906. The third son showed up: Philip. He was the darling of the family. But when he was thirteen, he died, a victim of the terrible Influenza Epidemic of 1919.

New life was just the thing to break our grief. And on November 24, 1920, Lyla was born. At last, a girl. Larry would come home from his sprouting career in vaudeville and play her bedtime stories on the violin.

From some of the old family stories, you'd think that Larry sprang from the womb with a straw hat and a cane. He was certainly knocking 'em dead on Third Street. By the age of two, he was entertaining Dad's customers by dancing on the jewelry counter. In fact, one time, he was dancing so hard that he crashed right through the glass and wound up crying among the diamond rings. There was no harm done, though: no cuts or bruises, just a surge of adrenalin for everyone present.

Larry even began playing the violin at the slaphappy age of four. But it was the result of a nearly tragic accident. Here's what happened:

Larry was playing in the store. Dad was bent over his workbench, testing for gold with oxalic acid. He'd dab a droplet of acid onto the metal, and if it dissolved or turned green, it wasn't gold. Gold stayed gold: it was immune to the acid.

Larry was playing explorer, adrift among the all-too-familiar objects. Finally, he landed the anchor of his nose on the alien land of Dad's work-bench. What a vista of weirdness! He grabbed an uncorked bottle. What was it? Soda pop? Ambrosia? It was the acid.

In the corner of his eye, Dad caught a glimpse of his son preparing to take a swig of this stuff that melts iron. He struck it from his hand. It was just in time, but some of the acid got on Larry's arm. The acid could tell right away that Larry's arm wasn't made of gold. Dad washed it off as well as he could and rushed his howling boy to the hospital.

Larry's arm was badly burned. One doctor, in fact, suggested amputating it. Always get a second opinion. Surgery and skin grafting saved his arm with minimal scarring.

A round of violin lessons was prescribed as therapy. Leading a bow through strings was just the kind of gentle exercise his arm needed. Swinging a baseball bat, for example, would have been too much exertion.

One of my earliest memories is of a scrawny, blond kid sitting in bed, slowly sawing away on a quarter-size violin, only eight inches long. He loved it. And he played it constantly.

Constantly.

Sometimes I think of Larry, Philip and me as the original Three Stooges. Larry was the instigator. Philip was the patsy. And I was the stooge in the middle who got blamed for everything.

One of our favorite routines was a black-face bit called "Playing in the Coal Bin." In those days, Philadelphia grocery stores had coal bins outside. And people would bring their buckets and scoop up as much as they could afford that day. We'd show up sometimes and just scrounge around in the bin on the way home from school. Instantly, we'd be a mess, and the storekeeper would be encouraging us to move on, complaining we were walking off with half his profits. "Walking To School" was usually good for a thrill. Co-staring with us in this routine were some tough Irish kids. See,

(l. to r.) Morris, Philip, and Louis (Larry Fine) Feinberg, ages 7, 5, and 9 respectively, 1909.

13

we lived in a neighborhood where there were ethnic differ-ences. And we had to go to a school that was quite a distance away. The Irish kids would wait for us. Of course, if we got in the schoolyard, we were safe. But if they caught us in the street, all hell would break loose.

Another great bit was "Sitting Still At The Dinner Table." This one started slowly, with a squirm here and a suppressed giggle there. But every so often, we'd work it up to a full-fledged food fight. We never threw any pies, though. Pies, we respected.

HUMORESQUE

Larry's first real performance was as a violinist at a chil-dren's concert with the Philadelphia Orchestra. Larry was nine years old. And he did the solo on "Humoresque," a Late Romantic piece by the Czechoslovakian composer, Anton Dvorak. Mother and Dad were ecstatic.

Some of you will recall "Humoresque" as the tune to Oscar Brand's outrageous lyric:

Larry, Moe, & Curly from *Disorder in the Court* (1936).
(from the collection of Steve Cox)

14

Passengers will please refrain   ·
From flushing toilets while the train
Is standing in the station, I love you.
We encourage constipation
While the train is in the station,
Moonlight always makes me think of you.

Mr. Brand's song, incidently, is a good example of what the French used to call a "vaudeville" in the 18th Century. Back then, a "vaudeville" (pronounced: vode-VEEL) was a satirical verse set to a well-known tune.

Like a family name, the word "vaudeville" changed dramatically in sound and meaning when it crossed the Atlantic and hit the Melting Pot.

RAGTIME ～～～～～～～～～～～～～～～～～

Our wind-up Gramophone in the living room sounded a sassy new note to Larry's career as a violinist. One of his friends brought over a ragtime record, and Larry was electrified. "Roll over, Beethoven," they say today.

Larry was first violinist in the orchestra at Southwark Grammar School, and his violin teacher had high hopes for him to become a concert violinist. But by the age of 13, he was sneaking off to music publishers to get ragtime sheet music and teaching some of his orchestral friends to play it. His teachers viewed this with alarm. His violin teacher nagged him to stick to the classics, and Larry started thinking of quitting the orchestra altogether.

Mother and Dad wanted Larry to continue with his violin lessons and become a serious musician: a classical musician. Dad, actually, had a vested interest, because he was a musician himself. He was always coming home with some kind of brass horn: a trombone, a trumpet, even a tuba. He'd play it all night sometimes, driving us all crazy. After a while, he would tire of it and sell it. Then, maybe months later, he'd buy a new one. What he wanted for his son was what he couldn't or wouldn't do himself: to get serious about it. Larry did get serious, but in a way that Dad didn't recognize at first. He entered vaudeville.

The door to vaudeville was amateur night. It was a friendly door, kindly to strangers and strangeness, and fat with prizes.

Larry as a somewhat older Buster Brown in *Quizz Whizz*
with Milton Frome & Joe Besser (1957).
(from the collection of Steve Cox) © 1984 Columbia Pictures Industries
Inc.

Entertainment was a prized commodity back then. Even
amateur nights packed the theaters. And even amateur
nights paid well enough for a kid and his violin, dreaming
their way to stardust. Sometimes first prize went as high as
$25. But the typical fare was treasure enough, ranging from
$10 to $2.50 for first through third prizes.

No big deal, you say? Let's haul out the old Sears-Roebuck
Catalog and see what that would buy.

Third prize would pay for four 14-carat gold rings or one
"double action automatic police revolver." Today, you'd need
hundreds of dollars to get into that much trouble.

Second prize could make you the happy owner of an over-
stuffed Turkish couch. A kid Larry's age could outfit himself
in a three-piece suit for such a princely sum.

First prize would buy a state-of-the-art sound system, complete with horn, crank, and a dozen records.

Larry had a lot of confidence in himself as a ragtime musician. But he was shrewd enough to want a gimmick. He was

small for his age, about four feet two inches tall, so he dressed to look younger. He wore a Buster Brown outfit: a broad-brimmed hat with a dangling ribbon, short pants, an oversized black bow tie. Everyone thought he was maybe seven or eight years old.

He could do anything he wanted. He sang; he danced. He played *Maple Leaf Rag;* he played *My Old Kentucky Home.*

Everyone thought he was a prodigy.

MINSTREL BOY ～～～～～～～～～～～～～ *1915*

Larry and I were backstage, talking to a wiry, frantic fellow with a notepad. Larry was getting signed up for that night's amateur show. I was carrying the violin: it wasn't a hard job, but theater managers figured it was worth a free admission.

The man with the notepad gave Larry a hard look. "Make sure your hair's slicked back nice and neat tonight, kid. I think Emmett Welsh is going to drop by. He's looking for someone like you."

Emmett Welsh was one of the last minstrel show impresarios in Philadelphia. In spite of the rising popularity of vaudeville, Mr. Welsh had chosen to preserve its ancestor.

Before the Civil War, minstrel shows — white performers in blackface singing and dancing simplified images of black culture — were the dominant force in show business. They played everywhere from the White House to California bars in the Gold Rush. In the 1870s, their scope expanded to include caricatures of the multi-national wave of immigrants that was beginning to arrive. The production numbers became

The logos Larry designed for himself and used on his stationery.

more lavish, parodies of circuses, in a widening search for more exotica to lampoon.

They were, of course, disreputable, although not for reasons we would imagine today. Nearly all popular entertainments were held to "reek of the saloon" by refined society. So it was to be with vaudeville as well.

By 1915, the minstrel shows had long since ceded their more ambitious production goals to vaudeville and were back to the basics of banjo and blackface. In Philadelphia, Dumont's Minstrels were closing their theater on 8th and Arch and splitting up. But at the last moment, Emmet Welsh appeared. He bought the theater, and the troupe was now Welsh's Minstrels.

Ever since the old Stephen Foster days in the 1850s, music publishing was an important and occasionally prestigious part of the business. So Mr. Welsh ran off a few of his own compositions and started "Emmett Welsh Music, Inc." What he wanted now was a little show that he could take around to local theaters to sell the songs. A show with a few gimmicks, maybe a kid violinist....

Larry looked presentable enough that night. His bow tie was on straight, and if his hair was a little mussed, most of it was under that Buster Brown hat of his, anyway. But there must have been some rosin built up on the 'E' string or something: *Maple Leaf Rag* squeaked like a bat. When he slumped offstage, he was nearly in tears. I grabbed the violin and put it in its case before he could throw it at the wall. Sometimes violin carriers come in handy!

Usually, we waited around to hear the emcee announce the winners, but a prize didn't seem to be in the cards. We decided to go home.

Standing at the backstage door was the dark shape of a man, a silhouette with bushy hair. "Larry Fine, is it?" he said. "Let me guess: that would be short for Feinstein, wouldn't it?"

"Feinberg."

"Tell me," said the shadow at the door, "does your violin usually squeak like that?"

"Hey, I won five bucks here a couple weeks ago!"

"Good," said the bushy-haired darkness. "I'm Emmett Welsh. I can use you."

So Larry went to work for Emmett Welsh, plugging songs all over Philadelphia.

But a kid violinist wasn't the only novelty that Mr. Welsh had in mind for this act. He also wanted to project the words to his songs on a movie screen, so that the audience could sing along.

It was an act tailored for the movie house, a new and different kind of theater, more novel than video game parlors are today. Two or three years earlier, the only movies most people saw were one-reel shorts in the middle of vaudeville shows. In fact, the length of a "reel" of film — 1,000 feet to run for nine minutes — was determined because that was the length of the average vaudeville act. But in 1915, D. W. Griffith's *Birth Of A Nation* was released; Charlie Chaplin's *The Tramp* was released; movies were coming of age. And while Mr. Welsh's song-plugging act was too much of an advertisement to fit in with other vaudeville acts, it worked well as an extra added attraction to a motion picture show.

I made sure to keep my old job of violin carrier at my former salary. I would sit in the front row, with Larry's empty violin case on my lap, and watch the show. Here was what I saw:

After an initial cartoon or "special effects" film — say, a railroad chase — the house lights would rise, and Mr. Welsh's song-pluggers would appear. Two singers would run out from stage right; Larry and the piano player would emerge from stage left. The piano player lifted little Larry, dressed in his familiar Buster Brown costume, to the top of his upright piano. The singers took their positions at the heads of the aisles. The piano struck a chord; Larry played the melody. The singers marched up and down the aisles, singing away with Larry's violin. They established eye contact with the crowd to force them to watch the words on the screen and sing along.

It was pretty successful: people went out to the Five and Dime Stores the next day and bought Mr. Welsh's sheet music. Larry worked as a song plugger for more than a year and brought home two dollars a night.

But Dad didn't like the late hours that Larry had to work, and when Larry's grades began to plummet, Dad put a stop to song-plugging. It was a last ditch effort to get Larry to take school seriously.

Still, Larry had accomplished his first goal: he had held a steady job in show business. He was a professional.

CHARLIE CHAPLIN 〰〰〰〰〰〰〰〰〰〰

In 1916, Charlie Chaplin, the immortal tramp, picked up $150,000 for signing a piece of paper, a contract that promised still greater wealth: a $10,000 weekly salary to make movies for a studio named Mutual.

Chaplin was the world's first movie star. Never before could a performer be everywhere at once, and still the public was insatiable. Chaplin "look-alike" contests became as common as merry-go-rounds in amusement parks.

Chaplin fever hit Larry as well. He'd walk home from the movies with the snappy, penguin gait of Chaplin's tramp. He found a little bamboo cane and got the twirls and pratfalls down to a "T".

In time, he put together the whole outfit: cutaway coat, wing collar, the little derby hat. A friend gave him an old pair of pants. On Larry, they were baggy and too long. They were just right.

Larry looked himself over in the floor-length mirror in Mother and Dad's room, danced around his cane, and smiled.

"Well, Moe," he said. "Let's take this show on the road!"

Dad supplied the transportation. He was an easy mark: he always got a kick out of taking the family to amusement parks on Sunday afternoons.

I was the hairstylist, in charge of transforming Larry's strawberry blond locks into Chaplin's black frizz. Burnt cork was my secret. I burnt the tips of a handful of corks and rubbed the ash into his hair. And presto: a mop of black curls. Turning Larry back into a blond was a far grimmer task.

But Larry was terrific in the Chaplin contests. He won often, even against grown-ups. He was so natural that even when his cane went spinning off into the crowd, people thought it was just part of the act. And so it was.

Sometimes when I watch The Three Stooges on TV, I get a jolt from Larry's video-dark hair. And I see a sooty-haired Chaplin, waddling his way to victory at Woodside Park.

Let me tell you about Larry's career as a professional boxer. Yes, I said, "professional boxer."

As far back as I can remember, "the fights" had been a source of mystery to both Larry and me. That's where Dad went every Friday night: to "the fights." But he never seemed to come home with any scrapes or bruises.

"Don't worry, boys," he grinned. "I just watch."

That was reassuring, but it didn't stop the flow of questions. Who did the fighting and why? Why did they fight every week? Why did they let Dad watch? How could Dad tell when they were going to fight?

Dad patiently answered our questions every week, and the mystery cleared a bit. We even knew the names of some of the contenders: Benny Leonard, Ad Wolgast, Yankee Schwartz....

Now we wanted to come along. We wanted to see these Friday Night Fights for ourselves.

So one night, when I was about six, Dad took us along to the Broadway Athletic Center for our first good look at a crowd of grown men having fun. It was violent, chaotic, scary and unbelievably noisy. It was wonderful.

Dad started taking us fairly regularly, and we became the darlings of Dad's ringside buddies. They were always kidding around with us, buying us stuff to eat, sparring with us. They'd let us know when they were telling a dirty joke, but they'd go to elaborate lengths to prevent us from actually hearing it.

Before each bout, they'd ask us to pick a winner. Most of the time, I'd pick the same guy that Larry would pick. If Larry picked the right guy, Dad's pals would reward us with quarters, dimes, even dollars. If Larry picked the wrong guy, we wouldn't get anything.

It didn't take us too long to hit upon a scheme: if we each picked a different fighter, one of us would collect big, then, later, we could divide the earnings evenly. It was a great scheme, but it only worked for a couple of weeks.

As always, Dad caught on.

When Larry was nine or ten, his doctor decided that his injured arm could benefit from more strenuous therapy than stroking a violin bow back and forth. Of course, Mother, Dad, violin lessons and the seductive call of vaudeville would keep Larry sawing away at his music. And, of course, Larry's doctor had no quarrel with that. It was simply time to add something more physical to his therapy.

In fact, Larry's doctor was a little late. Larry already liked sports: he was a relay runner in school. And like every other kid, he played baseball all summer long.

But now, it was time to pick a special sport: a sport that he would want to concentrate a lot of time and energy on, a sport that would make maximum use of his arms. Tennis, say. Or golf. Larry chose boxing.

By the age of 14, Larry had become a real terror in the ring. I was taller than Larry at this point, but I sure didn't pick on him.

He had joined a local gymnasium and made friends with its manager, a boxing promoter named Philip Glassman. Mr. Glassman had taken him under his wing, and soon he was sparring with the best in the business. The guy who led the calisthenics training was Benny Bass, who went on to become featherweight champion of the world.

Sometimes, vaudeville theaters would raise all their backdrops and show a few amateur fights in the middle of their shows. And Larry fought in a few of those. But Mother and Dad were opposed to Larry boxing in public. So Larry adopted the name, "Kid Roth," and hoped for the best.

Dad found out, though. Another jeweler dropped by his shop and inadvertently blew the whistle: "Hey, Joe, I see your kid's going pro next weekend! He did pretty well against the Zimmerman kid last night. But do you really think he's ready for a pro match?"

Dad was furious. Larry fought his professional match and won. But Dad was in attendance. And at the end of the fight, he dragged an embarrassed Larry out of the ring by his ear.

It was his last fight. True, he had beaten his scheduled opponent, but when he and Dad left no one could say he was retiring undefeated.

"School Days, School Days,
Dear old Golden-Rule Days...."

Larry was singing his way down the sidewalk, as always. It was a few days after Hanukah, a few days before 1917.

He was going downtown to see if he could find a song to plug at one of his favorite music publishing houses. While some houses, like Emmet Welsh's firm, concentrated on theatrical song-plugging acts to push their wares, others sent a bunch of kids, each armed with a song, directly into the five and dime stores where the songs were sold. The kids would stand at the sheet music counters and sing their songs. It was the musical equivalent of newsboys shouting, "Extra! Extra! Read all about it!"

Larry was going on his usual trek from music publisher to music publisher, looking for songs to plug like a golf caddie looking for a golfer.

"School Days, School Days,
Dear old Golden-Rule Days...."

Larry just couldn't stop singing it. It was one of those songs that just stick in your mind all day, a twist on the Chinese water torture, till by the end of the day you want to chop off your head to get rid of it.

He was still singing as he swung open the door of the first publishing house on his list.

The office manager waved Larry off: "No songs today. See ya tomorrow." He was clearly intent on a conversation that he was having with a very important-looking guy: impeccably tailored, hair combed straight back in the New York style.

Larry was speechless. This office manager was one of those guys who could always find time to laugh at Larry's jokes. He was a real buddy. So now he was throwing Larry out of his office?

Before Larry could leave, the office manager suddenly turned around and looked him over, as if for the first time. "You read music, right?"

"You know I do."

"Great, said the office manager, fumbling through the pile of sheet music on his piano. "Let's see....Do this one," he barked, shoving a sheet to Larry.

"Uh, sure."

The office manager led him to a rehearsal room with the nervous eagerness of a tailor guiding a customer to the fitting room.

Larry was beginning to suspect that this wasn't going to be a normal song-plugging job. And when he looked at the song that he was given, he knew for sure that something weird was going on. If ever there was a song that didn't need plugging, this old hit from the turn of the century was it.

Alone in the rehearsal room, he stared at the sheet music and sang:

"School Days, School Days,
Dear old Golden-Rule Days...."

The well-dressed fellow who had so captivated Larry's music publishing friend was a New York producer named Ben Edwards. Although he was relatively little known, he had no trouble capturing the attention of show business insiders. His brother, Gus Edwards, was one of Broadway's most formidable talents as composer, performer and entrepreneur. Gus seemed to come up with hit songs with the prolific ease of a politician making promises. Among his hits were *By The Light Of The Silvery Moon* and the insidious *School Days*. But at the time, he was probably best known as the father of "kiddie vaudeville." He would take countless casts of children and propel them to stardom in such spectaculars as *Kid Kabaret, School Boys and Girls, The Newsboy Quartet,* and *The Newsboy Quintet.*

Now Ben Edwards was preparing to take his brother's legacy one step further with *The Newsboy Sextet.* And Larry was auditioning for it.

"School Days, School Days,
Dear old Golden-Rule Days...."

It certainly promised to be a class act, with lots of growth potential. Eddie Cantor, one of Gus Edwards's discoveries, already graduated to the immortal *Ziegfield Follies*. Georgie Jessel, another Gus Edwards original, was playing that Everest of vaudeville, New York's Palace Theater.

When Larry thought of Gus Edwards, he thought of yet another graduate of the "kiddie vaudeville" shows, Herman Timberg. Herman Timberg was Larry's idol: the ragtime violinist who could tell a good Yiddish joke. And he, too, had prospered in the nurturing hands of Mr. Edwards. At that moment, Herman Timberg was preparing for his last performance of *The Passing Show Of 1916,* featuring music by Sigmund Romberg and George Gershwin and produced by two brothers who were fast becoming the kings of Broadway, Lee and J. J. Shubert.

But the thing that Larry really admired about Mr. Edwards' minions was this: they didn't have to go to school. Sure, they had to sing about it. But they didn't have to actually go there: this was before the days of method acting. They drew their act from the stage itself.

Ben Edwards liked Larry and hired him. Larry liked Ben. And while he had no way of knowing whether or not Ben would match his brother Gus' achievements as a "starmaker," he knew Ben's show would be a better gig than song plugging in five and dimes or amateur nights.

The only problem was winning Mother and Dad's approval. Surprisingly, that turned out to be no problem at all.

"Is this what you really want?" Dad asked.

"You know it is, Dad."

"Well, then, go ahead...."

Larry was stunned. And so was I. Larry thought that Dad had been won over by the weight of Mr. Edwards' credentials. Or his connections. Or his brother's connections. I thought that Dad was just tired of fighting with Larry about school.

Whatever the explanation, Larry was home free. He was going to New York to work with a man who had the connections to make him a star. And he was leaving school.

All he had to watch out for was homesickness.

Homesickness turned out to be a fierce foe. After a few months singin' and dancin' with the Newsboy Sextet, Larry came down with the first cold that he had faced without Mother's chicken soup. It was a bitter experience: too bitter to tolerate. He left the show and came back home to recuperate.

Mother greeted him as if he were a wounded soldier in the great World War that America had finally entered.

I had missed him terribly during his brief absence and couldn't wait to get back to my old job as violin carrier and make-up man.

But Larry didn't have a job for me. He didn't even have a job for himself.

He thought that he had tried and failed in show business. He thought that, at the tender age of 14, he was all washed up, that never again could he even play an amateur night. He was depressed.

Now, Larry was probably the most carefree guy in the world. I had never seen him really depressed before. And, in fact, I've rarely seen him depressed since. So when his cold disappeared and he was still moping around, we got concerned.

Dad had the solution: "Larry, it's time you got a job. If you don't want to go to school, fine. If you don't want a show business job, fine. But there's a war going on. And you have to do something."

So Larry got a job at the Hog Island shipyard, where the Philadelphia Airport is today. A job as a rivet passer.

Some of you younger folks will wonder what a rivet passer was. In those days, they didn't weld ship plates together, they riveted them. A team of riveters worked together as an assembly line. There was a riveter, a holder-on, a rivet heater and a rivet passer or catcher. The heater man had a charcoal heater with bellows attached. When he got the rivet red hot, he grabbed it with a pair of tongs and tossed it. The rivet passer caught it in a cone-shaped bucket, a soundless megaphone with a handle. The rivet was passed, again with tongs, to the holder-on. It was his job to push the hot rivet through a hole in the ship plate. On the other side, the riveter riveted the rivet with a pneumatic tool.

This was the dawn of the assembly line, and Larry was gleefully stunned by this goofy machine with human cogs. Larry had never seen anything like the rivet assembly line. And his response was to spend the better part of the day regaling his colleagues with jokes about the work they were doing.

Was Larry good at being a rivet passer? Well, he got a chance to recreate the role in the 1940 Stooges film, *How High is Up?* In the film, he had to pass the rivets on the bones of a skyscraper, 20 stories up, rather than on a sea-level ship factory. But the idea was the same.

See it for yourself. All things considered, he was a better comedian.

Rivet passing was no more glamorous than school had been, but it clearly lifted him out of his depression. He became a walking joke book again, cracking people up at parties, social clubs, everywhere he went.

He was especially a hit at the beach. We used to go to Atlantic City for weekends during the summer, and Larry's exuberant clowning won him wide popularity. Even his bathing suit was funny.

In those days, swimsuits were more elaborate than they are today. Women had to wear bathing suits with little skirts. Bikinis were unthinkable. Men were not permitted on the beach with bare chests.

Larry wore a tank-top that celebrated ethnic schizophrenia. The front was emblazoned with the Hebrew word for "kosher." And the back bore the message: "Erin go brough," which means "Ireland forever." With his reddish-blond hair, his gift of gab and his storehouse of Jewish humor, the tank-top suited him well. The beach crowd nicknamed him "Kosher."

Back home in Philadelphia, he began playing amateur nights again, dancing the *kazotchka* in the Russian Jewish style. His rear hovered inches above the stage as if he were sitting on an invisible footstool. He'd kick a leg out in a horizontal salute, bring it back, then kick out the other. It was a difficult dance: the only way you could do it without falling over was to do it fast. But, Larry would do it and play *My Old Kentucky Home* on his violin at the same time. He seemed determined to be a one-man melting pot of disparate cultures.

He also quit his rivet passing job. Now that he had recovered his sense of show business, he realized that rivet passing was irrelevant to his chosen career.

Dad struggled manfully to keep him employed, though, and even gave him a job with his jewelry business. By day, Larry would stand behind the counter of the store, keeping Dad's customers entertained. And by night, he'd rehearse an act with some friends called "The Keystone Komedy Kwartette." The act was named in honor of Mack Sennett's wildly successful Keystone Studios, home of the Keystone Kops and the only movie studio to ever devote itself entirely to comedy shorts.

After a couple of months, though, Dad was finding it difficult to tell which was the Komedy Kwartette and which was his jewelry business. Dad was finally convinced that Larry's future belonged to the stage.

Dad gave Larry two weeks salary and an extra $100 bonus to leave the business world alone. And Larry lived up to his part of the bargain. He got a job right away as a violinist with Howard Lanin's Orchestra at the Roseland Dance Hall. And he was never again employed as anything else but an entertainer.

EARLY ROUTINES ~~~~~~~~~~~~~ *1918*

The Great World War continued to drag on. When America entered the fray, it was confidently assumed that the balance of power would shift dramatically in the Allies' favor, and our soldiers would be returning triumphantly in a matter of months. It didn't turn out that way. And all over the country, homesick boys in boot camps were grimly training to get shot at. They needed a little cheering up, and vaudeville came to the rescue.

At that time, vaudeville was almost solely owned and operated by B. F. Keith's United Booking Service. It was Keith who determined who got booked into which theaters.

Larry as a doughboy.

Keith wasn't completely without competition. A few independents such as William Morris and Marcus Loew were forever snapping at his heels. But it was Keith who controlled the big-time theaters.

The war, though, opened alternative venues to Keith's theaters: army bases. David Sablosky, a shrewd, independent agent, seized the opportunity to put together a military circuit much like today's U.S.O. And he hired Larry.

Larry liked Mr. Sablosky. For one thing, he really looked

the part of a wily, successful agent: tall, balding and mustachioed. He looked like Bud Abbott, of Abbott and Costello fame.

Mr. Sablosky's idea was to team Larry up with a girl partner, so they worked out an act with a girl named Nancy Decker. Larry was pleased with it, and they hit the road.

But the act didn't get very far. A young dancer named Mabel Haney convinced Miss Decker that she would be better off in Mabel Haney's "Haney Sisters" act. So in the middle of their tour, Larry found himself without a partner.

This forced Larry into the protracted process of finding a new partner. Actually, finding one was no trouble. It seemed like every week he had a new partner. But somehow the acts never seemed to click.

I remember one girl in particular, a cute dancer named Winona Fine: no, she wasn't related to us. I used to tag along with Larry when he went to her house to rehearse. I was the critic.

They didn't want to bill the act as "Fine and Fine," so they settled on "Fine and Dandy." The act wasn't so fine and dandy, though. And in a couple of months, it was consigned to Larry's growing pile of doomed partnerships.

Through it all, when nothing else was working, there was always amateur night. Larry made a violin from a cigar box, a broom handle and a single violin string. He played it like a cello, holding it between his knees. It was a great gimmick for amateur nights, and he got some pretty sweet music from it. He won regularly.

At this point, of course, he wasn't really an amateur anymore. But as Larry liked to point out, "a lot of professionals aren't very professional either."

"Just you watch, Moe," Larry always said. "One of these days, I'll be playing the Palace."

Most of the time, it was a joke. He'd be complaining to me about an act of his that wasn't going right, then he'd stop and look at me with his impish grin and shout: "Next stop: The Palace!" And we'd fall down laughing.

He was serious about it, though. The Palace Theater in New York was the pinnacle of vaudeville, where a headliner could earn a thousand dollars in a single night. It was where the Gods of show business played; it was the Seal of Immortality. It was the Big Time.

But just now, Larry was playing the Girard, on Eighth and Girard in Philadelphia. Once a week, they put on an affair called "Discovery Night," or "Meet The Professionals," or even, "Celebrity Night." It was really a glorified amateur night. But rumor had it that the audience was crawling with booking agents looking for new acts.

"Class touch," thought Larry. "I like that."

Larry had given up on the idea of a girl partner and was trying to break in a single act. And the Girard seemed a pretty good place to do it. Sometimes agents were there; sometimes they weren't. But the real reason he liked playing the Girard was that he liked the guys who owned it: Jack Roof and Lew Ross.

Theater owners are usually businessmen, primarily interested in showing a profit. They may holler, "The show must go on!" But they aren't invoking the sentimental tradition of old troupers. They're announcing their reluctance to give refunds.

The Barons of the Girard, though, were comedians, real theater people. I got to know them pretty well myself. They always laughed at our jokes. Or rather: mine, they laughed at. Larry's, they used in their act.

They had a repertory company that used to do comedy revues — usually made up of routines stolen from musical comedies. Between scenes, the curtains would close, and while the stagehands shuffled props about, Jack Roof and Lew Ross would come out and tell a few jokes.

Jack Roof was the Irish guy. His "roof" was a flaming red fright wig, cut in the "Buster Brown" style. Lew Ross was the Jewish comedian. He was less clownish to the eye, but his jokes were fearless: ethnic and ribald.

Telling jokes during scene changes was an old vaude staple known as a "blackout bit." Originally, vaudevilleans would just turn off the lights and change the scenes in the darkness. But that was hard on the stagehands and tiring for the audience. So instead of a "blackout," they started closing the curtains and having a comedian or two come out to do a "bit" for the restless crowd.

Sometimes, they could change a scene just by lowering a backdrop, and a "blackout bit" wouldn't be necessary. They'd fade the lights for a few seconds, lower the backdrop, and presto: a new environment would be created.

The Girard had three backdrops and a curtain, and they defined the geography of the stage. If you did a "blackout bit" in front of the curtain as Roof and Ross did, you worked on "one." If you did an act before the first drop, you worked on "two." Acts before the second or third drops were on "three" or "four." A boisterously choreographed chorus line might have used "full stage," with no backdrops at all.

At this point, Larry's own act was a "blackout bit" — just Larry and his violin out there on a string of one-liners and a prayer.

JULES BLACK 〰〰〰〰〰〰〰〰〰〰〰 *1919*

It was a dark summer's night, overcast with hints of impending thunder and rain. Larry and I had just emerged from *The Cabinet Of Doctor Caligari*, the world's first horror movie, and were on our shaky way home. The drunken laughter issuing from the taverns seemed far more menacing than it ever had before.

The Girard was on our way, and we decided to drop by, just to say hello.

"Well, if it isn't the Feinbergs," bellowed Jack Roof as we snuck in through the backstage door. "Come on in. There's someone I want you to meet."

He introduced us to a roly-poly vaude veteran named Jules

Black. Jules was in his sixties, but his hair was thick and dark. And he was as vigorous as a man in his forties. He resembled a short Jewish Ronald Reagan, blown up like a balloon.

"Larry's the guy who worked with Ben Edwards. Calls himself 'Larry Fine.' He's got a great violin act, and he's up to here with jokes."

Jules Black was putting together a school act much like the Edwards brothers' shows, but on a smaller scale. No one was going to get rich from it, but Jules had lots of connections, and the work would be steady.

"You look good, kid. I want you to audition for me."

"Who else you got in the act?" Larry wanted to know.

"You probably don't know them," said Jules, "but let me tell ya: they're first class. I got Jolly Joyce; he does this German dialect. He's very funny. I got a great tenor, kid named Eddie Huskins. All the ladies wanna adopt him. Marty Bohn and Nancy Lee do a great song and dance. I got the Haney Sisters; they're..."

"The Haney Sisters?" Larry was stunned. "Is there a girl named Nancy Decker with them?"

"No, just Mabel and Loretta. They're really sisters, you know. You know 'em? They're a class act."

Larry smiled his smile of mischief. I could tell he was really interested in sharing the bill with the girls who had lured his best partner away from him.

"Hey, yeah," he said. "They're great. Hey, I'd love to audition for ya. When do we start?"

GOOD NEWS ~~~~~~~~~~~~~ *1919*

Dad and Larry both had good news to tell the family. But it was one of those situations when everyone's news, all told, clashed and the "goodness" of it drained away a bit.

Dad went first. He had gotten together with three partners and bought out a pawn shop in Atlantic City. The previous owner was ready to retire and wanted a nice little nest egg. It looked like a good business, so Dad decided to help him out. Dad was in the wholesale diamond business by this time, and he was earning enough to be on the lookout for all kinds of investments. But when Dad and his pals went to

Atlantic City to examine their new acquisition more closely, they realized they had made a shrewder deal than they could have known. There was so much stuff — valuable jewelry and art objects that were tucked in out-of-the-way places that never made it to the itemized inventory — that it seemed as if they had bought two stores for the price of one. It was a bonanza.

They had decided to mix business with pleasure. They would sell all the diamonds wholesale, which would cover their original investment and more. Then they wanted to gather their four families together and spend the rest of the summer — five weeks or so — in Atlantic City, playing on the beach and auctioning off the rest of the stuff.

Larry and I knew that this plan was heavy with emotional weight. Our dear brother Philip had died at age 13 of influenza only six months earlier, and we were old enough to see that this planned vacation was Dad's effort to heal the family, to bring us back together and out of our grief.

So it was with some trepidation that Larry announced his "good news." He had passed his audition and had been offered a steady job in Jules Black's "School Days" act. Jules Black himself wanted to drop by the following night to discuss the job with Mother and Dad. It was an old-fashioned gesture, and Larry hadn't liked it much when Jules first suggested it. After all, Larry was almost 17 and in control of his own destiny. But now, Larry was grateful: it meant that Jules could personally assume some of the responsibility for what Larry had to say next.

The act was going into rehearsal the day after tomorrow. And Larry wouldn't be able to go to Atlantic City. Depending on the schedule, he might be able to get away for a day or so, but....

Well, it was up to Mr. Black.

Jules Black turned out to be equal to the challenge of making Mother and Dad feel good about the act. He promised to take good care of Larry and look over him like a son, as he did for all the young people in his troupe.

Larry winced at this, but I was the only one who noticed.

Jules wound up the discussion by assuring Mother and Dad that he would work the schedule so that Larry could spend at least a week with us in Atlantic City.

Mother and Dad were totally charmed, and Jules was to become a good friend of the family.

The Atlantic City trip was a success as well. We all had lots of fun — even auctioning things off was more a party than a job. And Jules Black was as good as his word: Larry arrived for the last week or so, full of stories about his new act.

SCHOOLDAYS 〰〰〰〰〰〰〰〰〰 1919

For the first quarter of the century, after Gus Edwards proved the potential of kid shows, the country was treated to a swarm of school acts. In 1919, there were 50 of them playing B.F. Keith's big-time circuit alone. Beneath the notice of the monolithic Mr. Keith were at least another hundred, scraping by from one ramshackle theater to another.

One thing that made this type of show so widespread was that they cost very little to put on. You didn't have to pay the talent much: the cast was almost always unknown and under voting age. Whenever they got too old, you replaced them. And the props were incredibly simple for a full-length show. In the middle of the stage was a teacher's desk with a row of students' desks protruding from either side. The students faced the teacher with their profiles to the audience. And that was it: no scene changes; no fancy backdrops.

The shows would always be structured as a frenzied school day, from roll call to closing bell. And the students would make all the classic wisecracks that most kids didn't have the nerve to make in real life. Frequently, the teacher had to leave the room, and, under the guise of misbehaving, the "students" could do their song and dance numbers as well. The net result was primitive musical comedy.

Jules Black had been doing this kind of act off and on for almost 20 years. And while the script probably hadn't changed much in all that time, Jules liked to tell people that his new show was his best school act yet.

Jolly Joyce, heavyset and in his mid-twenties, was the teacher. He affected a thick German accent and a comically overbearing manner reminiscent of the Captain in the popular comic strip, *The Katzenjammer Kids.* He was the center that held the show together, and the pompous presence he established as he meticulously prepared to call the roll was the perfect set-up.

37

Larry was the first student on Jolly's roll call. "Absent!" he would say, when his name was called. "I'm sick in bed with a headache."

Jolly would give him an even worse headache by bopping him on the head with a stick. He didn't hurt Larry, though. He used what was known as a "slapstick" — two long, flat sticks, joined at one end like a castanet, that made a loud, cracking sound when he snapped them in the air. The "slapstick" never actually touched its victim, but it looked and sounded as if it had scored a direct hit. And Larry played it up: "Ow, ow, ow," he'd whimper. He was the sissy kid, the smart-alecky Little Lord Fauntleroy type.

Larry was the kid at the end of one row of desks, and Jules Black was the "kid" at the end of the other. Jules played the wise-cracking Jewish guy with an accent as thick as the one Jolly used.

Here's how they sounded:

Teacher: "Bubils, vot did Kristofer Kolumbis do in 1492?"
Jules: "I don't know, techer. I vas oud of town dat veek."

It might seem odd for Jules Black to be playing one of the kids, but it worked. Jules was as short as Larry and frantic with energy. He wore the same exaggerated school boy costume that Larry and the rest of the boys wore: short pants, black stockings, jacket and a giant bow tie that extended beyond the lapels almost to the shoulders. And he would cap all that off with a clownish wig with curls that fell just below the ears. He'd get a laugh just by walking onstage.

On Jules Black's side of the stage, between Jules and the teacher, sat two other students: Marty Bohn and Nancy Lee. Marty played the little tough kid, the class bully. With his hair slicked straight back, he looked like a junior Edward G. Robinson. But when the teacher left the room, Marty would sometimes relax his sneer and do a dance number with cherubic Nancy Lee.

Eddie Huskins and the Haney Sisters sat on the other side of the stage, between the teacher and Larry. Eddie was only 14, the youngest of the troupe, and didn't have much to do during the comedy bits. But when it was time for him to do a few songs, his beautiful tenor voice brought down the house.

The Haney Sisters, Mabel and Loretta, didn't get to tell

many jokes either. They were the innocent victims, foils for the boys' wisecracks and and pranks. Here's an example:

Teacher: "Vill vun uf the gurls gif us a pome?"
Loretta: "Snow, snow,
       Beautiful snow.
       Once I was pure
       As the beautiful snow."
Larry: "Yeah but you fell in the mud, kid."

As with Eddie Huskins, they got the last word when the show waxed musical. They did a delightful song and dance like twin Shirley Temples.

Larry was impressed. Sometimes, he'd tease them a little about stealing his old partner, but his heart wasn't in it.

"It sure is hard to stay mad at a couple of pretty girls," he'd say.

So he gave up and fell in love.

BACKSTAGE BANTER ~~~~~~~~~~~ *1919*

Jules Black's *School Days* ran for five years, touring all over the Northeast. I often went to visit them when they were playing eastern Pennsylvania or New Jersey. I even went as far as Dover, Delaware and the Folly Theater in Brooklyn to catch their act.

The act itself rarely changed much, but their offstage act was something else. The whole cast was a constant source of jokes and foolishness, and they had accepted me as "one of the gang" from the beginning. In some ways, I had the best of both worlds. I didn't have their tiring task of doing two or three shows a day, but I got to share their giddy, backstage pleasure at having just earned the crowd's applause. For me, it was like joining a party on wheels.

All parties breed gossip, and the school act was no exception. Onstage, the act was pure slapstick, but to us insiders, there were growing hints of romance. Marty Bohn and Nancy Lee had been dating even before joining the act. And everyone knew it was just a matter of time before they signed their legal names, Marty Cohen and Nancy Edelson, to a marriage license and became Mr. and Mrs. Cohen. But, the pair that really set tongues wagging was none other than Mabel Haney and our own Larry Fine.

Larry was always enthusiastic about the ladies, and Mabel was stunning: blond and pretty as a starlet, fun-loving and sweet. They were nearly inseparable.

Mother and Dad were crazy about Mabel. She was Catholic, but that didn't seem to bother them a bit. They were always encouraging Larry to bring Mabel along when he had time off and could come home for a visit. Sometimes, Larry and Mabel would babysit for our newborn sister, Lyla, and Dad would tell them it was good practice for raising grandchildren. He even started introducing Mabel to his friends as his "daughter-in-law." Dad was a little ahead of the game, but I think Larry and Mabel were both pleased by his obvious blessings.

Of course, Larry was still a teenager, with a little fooling around to get out of his system.

One time, I went to see Larry and the gang while they were booked in Camden, New Jersey. Larry adored Chinese food, so Larry and I set off in search of a good Chinese restaurant. Along the way, Larry decided to call a girl that he had met in town to see if she wanted to come along with us. She did. And before long, Larry, his date and I were sipping wonton soup and joking about the carefree life of vaudeville.

Suddenly, the color drained from Larry's ruddy cheeks: Mabel had just walked in and caught sight of us. Our companion, according to Larry's frantic explanation, hadn't been his date after all, but mine.

I don't think that Mabel was convinced, but she graciously went along with it. What transpired later, when Larry and Mabel had a chance to chat privately, is forever lost to history.

BROKE-DOWN CARAVAN ~~~~~~~1925

It was half-past midnight on a Saturday night, and I had finally finished sweeping up and polishing the glass counters at my cigar store. It was my first taste of being in business for myself. I thought there was nothing left to do but lock up when the phone rang.

"Must be the wrong number," I thought. I picked it up anyway.

"I have a collect call for anyone from a Mr. Larry Fine. Will you accept charges?"

"Yeah, sure!" I blurted. "Larry? You OK?"

"Hey, Big Brother," came the cheery reply. "I got a little favor to ask."

Here's what had happened:

The *School Days* troupe had just finished a three-day run, Thursday through Saturday, in Reading, Pennsylvania. As usual, they were to be paid after their final show. But the manager was nowhere to be found, and the cash box was empty.

The ticket-taker had seen the manager leave with the money, but there was nothing strange about that. The manager took the receipts home with him every night. The hapless ticket-taker had assumed that they had already been paid. He assured them that nothing like that had ever happened before.

They tried calling the manager at his home, but there was no answer.

Now they were in a bind. They couldn't go back to their hotel rooms, because they had already checked out that afternoon. And they couldn't get back to Philadelphia, because they were broke. They were standing around in the bitter cold Reading railroad station, hoping for a miracle. And I had been elected to perform it.

They wanted me to wire them trainfare by Western Union at once. Then, I was to meet them at North Philadelphia Station and take them all home in my car.

Sending them the money was no problem: I had just enough to cover their fare and the telegraph charge. But driving all eight of them home in my one-seat car was another matter. The most it could hold — even with everyone packed together on everyone else's laps — was four people, including the driver. So I had to break it down into three trips: first, I took the girls, then Jolly, Marty and Eddie, and finally, Jules and Larry.

I thought that the last trip would be the easiest and the most fun, because I'd only have two passengers and Larry would be full of chatter. But I was wrong. There was an icy silence between them that seemed to pack the car more fully than a whole trainload of passengers. I couldn't wait to drop Jules off and ask Larry what the problem was.

"That so-and-so still thinks he can keep me and Mabel apart," said Larry, as we sped away from Jules' house. "He even says he'll dissolve the act if I don't quit seeing her."

41

"He wouldn't do that."

"I don't care if he does! Everytime I turn around, it's: 'God forbid you should get married,' or 'A Jew and a *shiksa,* it'll never last.' I'm sick of it."

"Get Dad to set him straight," I suggested. "He can't argue with Dad."

"Won't work, Moe. Jules is Orthodox. *Boy,* is he Orthodox!"

The sun was rising, and the bones were weary as we pulled up in front of our house.

Then it hit me: "You're really gonna marry her, aren't you?"

"You bet, Moe. Gonna get that girl if it's the last thing I do."

A MARRIAGE MADE IN VAUDEVILLE 〰〰 1926

The *School Days* act held together for another year, but finally, Jules was ready to retire.

"With talent like you got, you don't need an old man like me," he told "his kids."

It was a strange, new world where Jews married Catholics, but he was willing to make his peace with it. He gave Larry and Mable a hug: "You don't invite me to your wedding, I'll knock your block off."

Actually, the Jew didn't marry a Catholic: he married a Jew. Grandmother Lieberman, our mother's mother, insisted that Mabel convert to Judaism before she could approve the marriage. Mabel didn't mind: after five years with Jules Black, she felt more Jewish than most of her Jewish friends. And her parents hardly noticed: two of their daughters, Rose and Margueritte, were already married to Jewish men. So Mabel took some classes from our local synagogue, classes she passed with flying colors, and Grandmother Lieberman gave her blessings. She knew a good match when she saw one.

It was time for a party, the melting-pot boogie, the wedding woven by vaudeville.

It was Sunday — January 22, 1926. And the site of the reception was the most famous club in town, the one owned by Van and Schenck, heroes of the Palace and the Ziegfield *Follies.* The club was officially closed on Sundays. So we rented it and had the whole place to ourselves. The house band was our band for the day. And Gus Van, the heavyset guy with the thinning hair, even sang a few songs from their radio show, while wiry Joe Schenck accompanied him on piano.

The guest list was huge and varied, fat with Cohens and Kellys, Rileys and Rombergs: a Philadelphia League of Nations. We didn't want the Haneys on one side of the room and the Feinbergs on the other, so we made sure to mix them together in the seating arrangements.

The Haneys were a very outgoing breed and easy to get to know. All three of Mabel's sisters were in show business. Loretta, of course, was a terrific singer and dancer. Marguer-itte, another dancing sister, was married to a well-known vibraphone player — Joe Green of "Joe Green and His All-Star Trio." Larry was a big fan of his. And Rose was married to Harry Romm, a New York agent who booked for the B. F. Keith circuit.

Rose was sitting next to Uncle Nathan, Dad's brother who had preceded him to America and adopted the name, Fein-berg. She was positively exuberant, forever filling the wine glasses of whoever wandered by, and toasting the happy couple. But Uncle Nathan was feeling left out. It seemed as if every time he wanted to fill his glass, Rose had comman-deered the wine bottle.

"Come on, Uncle Nathan," Rose chirped. "Let's have a toast!"

"Maybe if I was sitting at another table, I could get a drink," was his sad reply.

I got an extra bottle for their table, and Rose and Uncle Nathan wound up getting along just fine.

Of course, the *School Days* crowd was there: it was their graduation. Marty and Nancy had devised an impressive skit that involved dancing over little hurdles and were ready to tour as a team. Jolly was going to work in a new trio. Eddie wanted to land a recording contract.

But at the moment, our differing backgrounds and hopes for the future were idle daydreams, and we were one family, dancing the traditional Irish and Jewish dances all night long.

Larry and Mabel had an unusual idea for a honeymoon: to get back to work.

Larry had written a musical act called *At The Crossroads* that he wanted to perform with Mabel and Loretta. Mabel was uncertain about it, so they decided to show it to their brother-in-law, Harry Romm, and see what he thought. Harry was an important man in the business, but they had nothing to lose. If he didn't like it, he'd be nice about it.

Harry Romm was a quiet fellow, short and rotund, not given to showy displays of excitement. But he was clearly impressed with Larry's script. In fact, he insisted on being their agent.

"When can you be ready?" was all he wanted to know.

It was an offer they couldn't refuse. Mabel cast off her doubts, and they told him they'd have the act together in a few weeks. There was a lot to do: scenery to build, costumes to make, and plenty to rehearse.

In the act, the Haneys were uniformed traffic cops at a fork in the merry road through Melodyland. Loretta directed traffic to the classical section, and Mabel pointed the way to jazz. Larry was the puzzled traveller in the middle of the road. Mabel lured him her way with a jazz dance which he gamely accompanied on his violin. Then Loretta led him back with a ballet which he also played for. Always agreeable, Larry wound up playing a violin solo that combined the two musics as the Haneys disappeared to change costumes. Then Larry left the stage, and the Haneys emerged in evening gowns to sing a duet. Finally, Larry came out in a tuxedo and joined them in a closing number.

In many ways, the piece was a symbolic autobiography of the pre-Stooge Larry Fine. It was a class act, lavish for vaudeville, and Harry Romm had no trouble getting them bookings.

In no time, they were well-established as a hot team. The theaters all sent excellent reports back to Harry Romm, and their billing and salary climbed steadily. They weren't playing New York's great Palace Theater. But they were playing the Palace in Cleveland and the Royal Theater in New York. They were getting close.

Mel Klee, a famous blackface comedian, got a big kick out of their act, and they all decided to work together. *At The Crossroads* required "full stage," so it was the closing act. Mel Klee worked on "one," as a single, so he was next-to-closing, driving the audience wild with laughter while the stagehands set the stage for Larry and the girls.

Mel was about ten years older than Larry and was the first well-known performer that Larry had appeared with. So he was a big influence. Larry studied Mel's act seriously, until he knew it as well as Mel did.

They played all over the Northeast and Midwest on B. F. Keith's Circuit and took a swing through the South on the Delmar Circuit.

"We did the Charleston in Charleston, South Carolina," he told me once. "We showed 'em how it's *really* done."

It was a good year for Larry. All of a sudden, he was married to the woman of his dreams and riding the wave of a hit act.

MOE FINE AND HAROLD FARR ~~~~~~ *1926*

Larry was doing so well in vaudeville that I decided to give it a try myself. Maybe some of his magic had rubbed off on me over the years. Besides, I was 21 years old, and everything's possible when you're 21.

So I worked out a comedy act with an old friend of mine, Harry Fairman. We had been kids together, and now we were going to do vaudeville together. He changed his name to Harold Farr, and we hit the road.

We used to do Jewish humor. Let me show you what I mean:

The man says to his wife, he says, "Close the window it's cold outside."

And she closes the window, and she says, "So now it's warmer outside?"

Here's another one we used to do:

The fella's walking along the street with his wife, and they're talking. And a blond walks by and says, "Hello, Sam."

And he keeps right on walking and don't say anything. She turns to him and says, "Sam, who's the blond?"

He says, "Don't bother me." Keeps right on walking.
She says, "Sam, who's the blond?"

He says, "Don't bother me." Keeps right on walking.

Finally she says, "Sam, you tell me who's the blond, or I'll knock your block off."

He says, "For God's sake, don't bother me. I'll have enough trouble explaining to her who you are."

The two of us would also do skits together. This was one of our favorites:

Harold would say: "I gave you a suit to take to the tailor, and I left my watch in the suit. When I went to get the suit back, the tailor said there was no watch. Give me back my watch."

Then I'd go into my "tears act." I'd say, "Are you accusing me of taking your watch? You and I went to school together when we was kids. And now you're accusing me of taking your watch?" And I'd start to blubber.

Morris Feinberg at age 21 near Strawberry Mansion in Philadelphia.

Finally, Harold would give up: "All right, forget it. Just forget it. I won't say anymore."

So I'd say: "Can I keep the watch now?"

We played small-time vaudeville houses. There were millions of them. We played in Philadelphia and the neighboring areas from Maryland and Delaware up to New York. We knocked ourselves out for a year or so, but we never made big time.

What finally killed the act was all the travelling we had to do. A little weekend trip to Atlantic City was one thing. But to survive in vaudeville, you had to be on the road seven days a week. And I really got fed up with it. I've hated travelling ever since.

If that was Larry's idea of a good time, fine. He was one of those odd creatures whose habitat was the open road. But my home was home.

THE CANADIAN CIRCUIT ～～～～～～～～ 1926

Vaudeville was the most mercurial business in the world. Acts would come together in one pattern, then rearrange themselves into another pattern overnight like images in a kaleidoscope. Now Mel Klee had gone off with another sister act, and bookings were starting to dry up. But before Larry could get discouraged, an attractive proposal came in the mail from Eddie and Dorothy Laughton.

Dorothy had been in the Haney Sisters act for awhile before the Jules Black days. But then she had married Eddie, a tall, handsome comedian with a pencil-thin mustache. Now they were in Toronto where Eddie was a popular emcee at the Paramount Theater. Would Larry and the Haney Sisters like to come out and be in his show? Eddie had heard good things about their act, and it would be fun to get together, reminisce about old times and catch up on each others' lives.

The Laughtons had timed their offer perfectly. In two weeks, the Haney Sisters and Fine were in Toronto, wowing the crowd at the Paramount.

Among the wowed crowd was Sol Burns, a friend of the Laughtons and a successful booking agent. After their open-

Eddie Laughton in the days when he appeared in Three Stooges' shorts such as *Three Little Beers* (1935) or *Movie Maniacs* (1936).

Larry (standing on the crate), Moe, and Curly in publicity for *Swing Parade of 1946.*

ing night show, he rushed up to Larry and offered them 15 weeks on the Canadian Circuit, from Toronto to Vancouver.

But Loretta had bittersweet news: she was engaged to be married and had to go back to Philadelphia after the Toronto run. "I wanted to tell you back in Philly," she said. "But I know how much this act means to you, and I thought I'd wait till after Toronto. I guess I just chickened out."

Larry and Mabel had a very special trait in common: they were the most easygoing people in the world. Loretta was breaking up their act just as they had been presented with a very lucrative offer. But they couldn't come up with a single cross word.

Good cheer and champagne was their reply.

Everyone had such a marvelous time in Toronto that when Loretta went back to Philadelphia to plan for the wedding, Larry and Mabel decided to spend a little more time visiting with the Laughtons.

Eddie was running an amateur night at the Paramount that

he wanted Larry to see for old times' sake.

Larry left a few hours early for the show so he could drop by another theater and catch a movie to steel himself for the ordeal.

Larry lost himself in filmland. The sultry blond was just about to surrender herself to the charms of Rudolph Valentino when it was time to change reels and Larry was presented with a rude surprise. The words, "Larry Fine wanted at the box office," flashed on the screen.

Visions of disaster exploded in Larry's head. He jumped from his seat and dashed to the lobby: "I'm Larry. What is it?"

"All I know is Eddie Laughton just called and wants you at the Paramount immediately."

Larry had another surprise in store for him when he went out into the cold Canadian night: the great blizzard of 1926 was in progress. The streets were already packed with snow, and it was still coming down with a vengeance. But concern led him on through the terrible storm, and when he got to the Paramount, he found an even more frantic Eddie Laughton.

"Listen, Larry," he said. "Half the acts can't make it tonight. We've been promoting this for weeks: first prize is a week-long run here at the theater. You know, the big time. It's going to look real dumb if no one shows. I need every act I can get my hands on."

"Hey, I'll do an act for ya, Eddie. It'll knock your socks off."

"Well, that's why I called you, Larry. But it won't work. Everyone knows you from last week. They'll know you're a pro."

Larry waved him off: "They'll never suspect a thing. Got any blackface?"

The proverbial light bulb went off in Eddie's brain: "Of course! Blackface!"

They ransacked a dressing room and came up with a half-full stick of the greasy stuff.

"Well, this is all I need, Eddie, my man. Just tell me when to go on."

Eddie was elated: Larry did Mel Klee's act word for word, nuance for nuance, and brought down the house. "No wonder

Mel's so famous," thought Larry. "This is great material."

The biggest problem came later, when it was time to pick a winner. Larry was clearly the favorite, but if he won, people would find out that he was a pro.

Eddie had the solution. At the end of the show, he lined up the contestants as expected and put his hand over each of them so that the audience could "vote" with their applause. But when he came to Larry and the crowd started cheering wildly, he moved his hand to the girl standing next to him. She won, and Eddie saved his job.

Eddie and Dorothy threw a gregarious party at their house that night. For such a snowy evening, the turnout was terrific. Most of the contestants showed up. And, according to Larry, a good portion of the audience came along as well. The important thing was that Sol Burns, the theatrical agent, was there.

"You know," Sol said, studying Larry, "if I didn't know you were in that sister act, I would have sworn that you were the blackface guy tonight. Who was that, anyway?"

"Search me," said Larry. "I'm new in town."

But Sol was sharp, and by the end of the evening, he noticed some bits of blackface left behind Larry's ears.

"You *were* the guy, weren't you?" Sol announced.

"Well, yes and no," admitted Larry. "Actually, it's Mel Klee's act."

"Well, no one knows from Mel Klee up here," said Sol. "And besides, I can't afford him. You, I can afford. I want you to do that 15 week tour I offered your other act. But I want you to do it as a single. What do you say?"

Well, what do you think he said? Mabel was all for it: she had heard about Larry's fine performance. And I think she enjoyed the idea of just coming along for the ride, without having to go onstage.

Larry's only stipulation was that he not use blackface. He'd do the Mel Klee routines in Larryface.

He was overjoyed, actually. Working as a single was a major breakthrough for him. He had always admired stand-up comics who went out there with no props, no violin, no partners and carried the show. Now it was his turn.

Larry was on top of the world when he called home to tell Mother and Dad about his new solo act. But Dad was strangely morose.

"How long is the run?" he wanted to know.

"Fifteen weeks to start," said Larry. "But Sol's already talking about signing me up for a whole year!"

"Well, I guess that means I'll never see you again."

"Don't be silly, Dad. A year isn't so long."

"You do a good job, Larry. Maybe I'll come out and see you."

It was an unsettling conversation — and sadly prophetic. The very next day, Dad died of a stroke. Larry was heartbroken. For the rest of his life, he would say that his greatest disappointment was that Dad hadn't lived long enough to share his success in show business.

Larry's tour wasn't slated to begin for another two weeks, so Larry and Mabel returned to Philadelphia to console Mother and poor Lyla, who wasn't even six years old at the time.

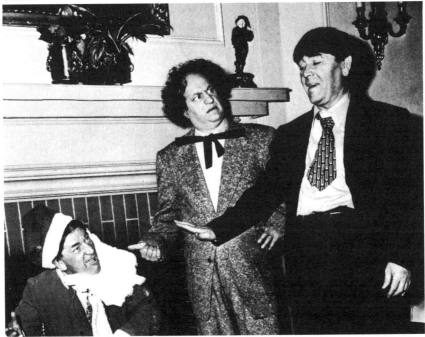

Shemp, Larry, and Moe from *He Cooked His Goose* (1952).

While in Philadelphia, they also contacted Loretta and found her full of surprises. She had had a fight with her boyfriend and wasn't getting married after all. Now she wanted to get back to work.

Larry was all set as a single and wasn't about to give it up for Loretta. But Harry Romm suggested that he could book the two sisters for the same money that they had been making as a trio. It was a good deal. So they finally agreed that Larry would do the 15 weeks in Canada and Mabel would go off and do the sister act with Loretta.

Larry was a smash hit in Canada, but after a couple of weeks on the road, he began to wonder how long he was going to be able to handle not seeing his wife.

He needn't have worried about it. Going on separate tours hadn't set well with Mabel either.

It was the week before Christmas. Larry was playing the Paramount in Saint Catherine, Ontario, and Mabel was in Chicago, working with Loretta at the Chez Pierre, "America's Most Beautiful Restaurant Theater." Mabel, a former Catholic, had many fond family memories of Christmas holidays. And she had come to the conclusion that she didn't want to spend her first Christmas as a married woman without her husband. So she called Larry and suggested he join her in Chicago, right away.

Larry was aghast: this tour had been his biggest break yet in show business. He couldn't just throw it out the window. What she was asking just wasn't possible.

"Talk to Sol," was her reply. "Tell him you're sick. Tell him your wife is threatening to leave you. Anything! This is important to me. Larry, please, come to Chicago."

Larry decided that maybe it was possible after all. He agreed to talk to Sol and try to work something out.

Now it was Sol's turn to be aghast: "I try to book you with your family act, and the act breaks up. I try to book you as a single, and you want to take a vacation. You want to be in show business or what?"

Luckily, Sol Burns was a good friend and not just another promoter. He wished him good luck and let him go.

Larry arrived in Chicago on Christmas day, and Mabel and Loretta threw a big bash for him at their hotel that night.

Larry hadn't felt so uncertain about his career since he had to leave the *Newsboy Sextet* act when he was a kid. But he had to admit that it was wonderful to see his young wife again.

Gigantic Christmas parties became a tradition with the Fines from that night on. In their Hollywood days, it was the hottest ticket in town among their crowd.

THE RAINBO GARDENS ~~~~~~~~ 1927

In the thick of the Roaring Twenties, Larry Fine found himself in Chicago, the city of gangsters and bootleg liquor, faced with the task of rebuilding his career. His first step was to do what came easiest to him: he made friends.

Several people at Mabel's Christmas party had mentioned a "Comedy Club," whose membership included not only local comics but agents and producers as well. It was just a social club, a place to relax with fellow show biz types, but the professional advantages seemed clear. He joined right away.

One day, Larry was playing cards at the Club — losing, as usual — with an interesting fellow named Fred Mann.

Fred Mann was the owner of an exotic establishment called the "Rainbo Gardens." Even the spelling of its name was unusual. It was a fronton — which might be loosely described as a cross between a racetrack and a casino. Like a racetrack, it specialized in an exciting physical sport. A fronton was an arena with a playing area five times the size of a tennis court for the game of jai-alai (pronounced "hi-li"). And the management gleefully accepted bets on the outcome of the games. Like a casino, it also housed a nightclub. After the games at the Rainbo Gardens, patrons could retire to the Rainbo Room to celebrate or console themselves with a top-notch floor show.

The Rainbo Gardens billed jai-alai as "The World's Fastest Game," but that was only half the story. It was also the most dangerous. With no protective padding and armed only with a long straw basket attached to one hand, a jai-alai player had to confront a rock-hard ball ricocheting off a wall at more than 150 miles per hour. The idea was to catch and throw the ball in one motion which sent it speeding back at the wall and toward the other player.

Larry had never seen a jai-alai game before. But he was an avid gambler, and he thought he'd feel right at home in the Rainbo Gardens. Fred agreed, and to further entice him, he launched into an eloquent description of the revue that was to open that night in the Rainbo Room.

But the mellow mood was shattered by the frazzled entrance of Fred's partner, LeRoy Prinz. LeRoy was the producer of the Rainbo Room, and he had grim news. Ray Evans, the show's emcee, had just quit in a dispute with the angel-voiced songstress, Ruth Etting, over who would get top billing.

"Let me talk to him," said Fred. "Where is he?"

"No one knows. He stalked out in a huff, saying he wouldn't be back."

Larry leaned forward a little: "Let me cover for this Evans fellow."

Fred was sadly shaking his head: "Do you sing? Can you sight-read a piece of music? You got six numbers to learn by tonight."

"Yeah, I can do all that stuff. And I play violin and do comedy."

"You told me you played cards, too," noted the world-weary Mr. Mann. "But are you any good?"

And so it was that Fred Mann and LeRoy Prinz found themselves frantically calling Harry Romm, Sol Burns and various theater owners to get the straight dope on an unemployed comedian and musician they hadn't heard of before that afternoon.

To their surprise, everyone gave him good notices. So they wished him luck, collected their winnings and sent him into frenzied rehearsal.

Larry learned his part quickly and even had time to watch a bit of a jai-alai game. One player in particular caught Larry's eye: a flamboyantly angry man who threw a tantrum whenever he missed a shot. Larry thought he was wildly funny, a real stitch, but the crowd didn't "get it." They were too engrossed in the drama of the game.

Larry was a pretty good last minute replacement that night. He performed the scripted material well enough to please LeRoy Prinz, the guy who put most of it together. But what really brought the house down was Larry's mimed burlesque of the furious jai-alai player he'd seen. To Larry, it was an off-hand improvisation, but it was a revelation to the crowd. The same gestures that had seemed such a perfect visual symbol of their excitement were now exposed, in this new setting, as totally hilarious!

Fred Mann was delighted and appointed Larry permanent emcee of the Rainbo Room. It was a good offer, fraught with more potential than anyone could have imagined.

Perhaps the old gypsy woman, who had stared so deeply into Fannie Lieberman's palm in the 1890s, was peering down from heaven to that Chicago night. If so, she would have smiled gleefully about what would happen next when Al Jolson, Ted Healy and *A Night In Spain* would come to town.

A NIGHT IN SPAIN ～～～～～～～～～～ *1928*

On Sunday, March 11, 1928, the big theatrical news in Chicago was the arrival of the great Al Jolson. For nearly two decades he had been the Superstar of his day: The King of Broadway, the man who could out-gross the Ziegfield *Follies* on a bare stage.

Once, during a run of the musical, *Big Boy,* he even stopped in the middle of the show and shouted: "Do you want me, or do you want the show?"

The crowd screamed, "We want Al! We want Al!"

Jolson dismissed the cast and sang a solo concert for the rest of the evening.

His producers, Lee and Jake "J. J." Shubert, made millions off of his untouchable magic. Jolson's appearance in the 1926 Chicago run of the Schubert musical, *Artists and Models,* led it to gross $60,400 in a single week, more than any other musical in history.

The Shuberts were well-known as penny pinchers: they regularly infuriated their stars by charging them for such things as paper cups used during rehearsals. One famous story had them charging Eddie Cantor $1,900 for glue used to make sets during a Shubert show in which he appeared. But even the Shuberts had no choice but to make Al Jolson the best paid star on the stage.

Ted & Betty Healy in *A Night in Spain.*
(Billy Rose Theatre Collection of the New York Public Library)

By 1928, theater itself was too small to contain him: he was
the star of *The Jazz Singer,* the first feature-length "talkie."
It was the hit movie that saved Warner Brothers from bank-
ruptcy and was changing the face of the industry.

Now the Shuberts were willing to pay Jolson the extra-
ordinary sum of $10,000 a week to cap the resurgence of
A Night In Spain in Chicago.

A Night In Spain had enjoyed a moderate success in New
York, opening in the spring of 1927 to amused reviews and
running through the summer. It was a loose musical comedy
with lots of pretty girls and only token plot elements. But one
thing that made the show stand out was the presence of a
madcap comic named Ted Healy, who performed with his

wife, Betty, and a man with the unlikely name of Shemp Howard.

"Healy," the *New York Times* had exulted, "is the funniest he has been since the vaudeville days." Even Healy's unkempt stooge, Shemp Howard, had won approval from New York critic Bide Dudley, "Shemp is what might be called a 'scream!' And the best part of it is it isn't a false face he wears on stage."

But a summer-long run on Broadway, while respectable, is not the run of a blockbuster hit. When it opened at Chicago's Four Cohens Theater in November, everyone gave it about six weeks to run, eight at the most. The long-running musical, *Good News,* hovered nearby, waiting to replace it at the first sign of the faltering ticket sales that never seemed to come.

Chicagoans were still merrily buying tickets to *A Night In Spain* after 15 weeks, but trouble loomed. Phil Baker — one of the show's stars, the accordianist who took all the comic abuse from his partner, Sid Silvers — either fell ill or out of sorts with the Shuberts, depending on whose gossip you believed. The Schuberts felt that there was still money to be made from their old Spanish war-horse, and they were taking no chances. They decided to replace Mr. Baker with the best in the business, the King of Broadway himself.

Chicago erupted in an orgy of ticket-buying.

THE AL JOLSON HANDICAP ∿∿∿∿∿ 1928

On March 24, two weeks after Jolson's arrival, the Rainbo Gardens hosted an "Al Jolson Handicap," a special midnight game in his honor. "Al Jolson in person and *Night In Spain* will be guests at Jai-Alai," proclaimed the ads.

The Rainbo Gardens was constantly headlining various stars in promotional games. They had Jolson on Saturday night, and lined up for Monday was a "Meek and Meek Handicap plus Six Other Thrills." After the game, Larry would host a party — much like today's "celebrity roasts" — for the honored guest in the Rainbo Room. This meant that he had to do a different show every night, but by now, Larry was churning them out with the graceful aplomb of a Johnny Carson.

But tonight was special. The place was packed and the air electric, as Larry sallied forth with his Jolson jokes.

Unknown to Larry, he was being seriously studied by an unlikely pair: Ted Healy and Shemp Howard from the cast of *A Night In Spain*. Larry had hardly noticed them in his concern over doing his Jolson imitation for Al Jolson himself. Actually, Jolson didn't pay much attention to Larry: he had seen Jolson imitations before. But Messrs. Healy and Howard were on the case.

Shemp wanted to leave *A Night In Spain* and was desperately searching for a replacement. Like everyone else, Shemp had thought the show would be closed by this point. So he had signed to do an act with Jack Waldron, another young survivor of the Shubert stage. But Healy was making it difficult for Shemp to quit. Shemp was Healy's stooge — the foil for Healy's jokes, the guy he beat on the head with his crumpled fedora. Healy didn't even want to consider a replacement. He had known Shemp and his brother, Moe, since they were kids in New York. How do you replace a boyhood chum?

But Shemp was persistent: "What about that Fine guy? He really knocks himself out up there."

Healy wouldn't hear of it: "To replace you? Are you nuts? He's too clean-cut."

Healy thought Shemp looked like a thug, dangerous and dumb, and it was just the look he wanted. Even though Shemp was only in his early thirties, his face had a curiously weather-beaten quality to it like a prizefighter's face or a cigar store Indian that had been used for target practice.

"Take him to see 'Aunt Matilda,' " Shemp suggested. "He'll look like hell in no time."

"Aunt Matilda" was Healy's code word for the next stop in a wild night of bar-hopping. "No one goes home until we've seen my dear, old Aunt Matilda," Healy would say. Then they'd go out into the night to look her up and find themselves in another speakeasy. Many a show-biz great had gone along with Healy on his eternal search for "Aunt Matilda," but few remembered what had happened next.

Healy shook his head: "He looks like a god damn *kid,* Shemp. If I shove him around onstage, they'll send me up for child abuse."

Shemp hung in there: "Look, you gotta admit he's the right size."

The bottom-line requirement for becoming a Healy stooge was this: you had to be short, so that Healy could tower over you. And Larry had that, at least, covered.

Healy was still shaking his head, but he didn't reply. He gave a five dollar bill to a waiter and asked for a double shot of bootleg bourbon, straight up.

Shemp couldn't stand it anymore: "Do what you want, Ted, but I'm leaving. What are you going to do, hold a gun to my head?"

"The thought did occur to me," said Healy.

But by the end of the show, Healy had decided that maybe this Fine character wasn't so bad after all. He was funny enough and seemed to be able to improvise well.

So Healy called Larry over to his table and got straight to the point. "Hey, fella," he said, "how'd you like to be in *A Night In Spain?*"

"Why? Jolson's not good enough for ya?"

Larry, of course, thought Healy was just kidding around with him, and for a while, the two just traded barbs. But as the conversation wore on, and Healy started explaining the part to him, Larry decided that Healy might actually be serious about this offer.

"Well, I do have a contract with this place," said Larry.

"You what?" Healy was incredulous. "Look, I'm trying to do you a favor. My friend Shemp, here, says maybe you're not ready for the Big Time. But I said, 'No, no: the boy's got talent. Let's give him a break.' What do you say, fella?"

"Wait a minute!" Larry protested. "I haven't even seen the show yet. Let me come by on Wednesday afternoon and watch the matinee. Then I'll see what I can do."

"Well, all right," said Healy. "I just hope the spot's still open by then. I'd sure hate to see you throw it all away in this dump, being some kind of glorified maitre d' all your life."

Larry was speechless. It was true that he wasn't really getting anywhere by staying at the Rainbo Gardens. And worse, he was giving most of his earnings back to Freddie Mann at the jai-alai games. What if Healy were on the level?

"See you Wednesday afternoon," said Ted Healy.

If Larry was worried about how a Yid from Philadelphia was going to seem Spanish enough to blend into an exotic *Night In Spain,* his concerns were laid to rest at the Wednesday matinee. Aside from the costumes, there was a good deal more Chicago than Madrid in the show. Twenty of its 32 scenes made no reference at all to Spain. While the leggy Gertrude Hoffman Girls may have been the "most beautiful senoritas in the world," as the ad had it, there was a distinct American showgirl quality to them. And when Jolson came on to do his *schtick,* the show might as well have been called *A Night On Broadway.*

Ted Healy wasn't even in costume. He just wandered on stage in his street clothes like a brash bum crashing a Society Ball. He jammed a bunch of eggs down Shemp's throat, tackled showgirls by the neck, made disparaging comments about the show, commandeered the orchestra, and made a shambles of whatever pretensions to civility the show may have had.

The beautiful ladies of the chorus from *A Night in Spain.*
Photo by De Mirjian (Billy Rose Theatre Collection of the New York Public Library)

The audience ate it up. Larry wondered if you got combat pay to share the stage with that madman.

Either way, his mind was made up: he wanted to do the show. And as it turned out, nothing at all stood in his way.

When Larry arrived at the Rainbo Gardens to negotiate an end to his contract, the place was padlocked. Large signs were haphazardly posted all over the front of the building, and their message was this: "This Establishment CLOSED by the Internal Revenue Service." The Rainbo Gardens had been raided by the watchdogs of Prohibition.

Larry got to a phone booth and tried to get through to Fred Mann, but he was unavailable, in conference with his lawyers. So he got in touch with LeRoy Prinz, who filled him in on the details.

The situation wasn't really as bad as it looked. It was just a few waiters trying to supplement their incomes by selling booze. There was no evidence that anyone else was involved. The lawyers thought they could get the jai-alai fronton, the gaming arena, back up quickly — perhaps by tomorrow. But the Rainbo Room was another matter. No one was even guessing when the nightclub could reopen.

Larry hailed a cab and went straight back to the Four Cohens Theater. He was free to seek other employment, free to join *A Night In Spain*.

Fortunately, Healy and Shemp were still there. Healy was on the phone to someone about an Actors' Fund benefit he was to emcee that Friday afternoon. Shemp, of course, was delighted with Larry's news. And when Healy got off the phone, he suggested that Larry catch the evening performance from the wings, to get more of a feel for the show.

Up close, the raucous revue was a study in total chaos: every five minutes or so, there was another scene change, another tumult of exiting and entering acts. It was a real chore to stay out of everyone's way.

At one point, Al Jolson was standing right behind him. "I never got a chance to watch the show before," he told Larry.

Larry was carelessly laughing at Ted Healy's antics when Healy suddenly stopped in his tracks and signaled to Jolson. Jolson gave Larry a hard shove, and suddenly, Larry was onstage before a capacity crowd, with no idea what was going to happen next.

Larry, Curly, and Moe.
(from the Jane Howard Hanky Collection, courtesy Steve Cox)

Moe, Curly, and Larry on the bandstand in *Swing Parade of 1946.*

STOOGE ACTS

Larry felt like an idiot as Healy let loose with his full barrage of physical and verbal humiliation. From time to time, Healy would feed him a line under his breath, which Larry would loudly repeat. But that would just lead to another joke at Larry's expense.

The audience responded warmly to what they perceived as Larry's convincing portrayal of a man half ready to wet his pants with stage fright. It was the kind of routine that, decades later, the comedian Don Knotts would make a staple of his act. After what passed as a jolly few minutes to the audience and a tortured eternity to Larry, Healy and Larry left the stage to heated applause.

A chuckling Al Jolson gave Larry the thumbs up sign: "Lookin' good," he said.

"You went over great out there," Healy agreed. "Now let's get together with Shemp and go over what we're gonna do after intermission."

"After intermission?" Larry screamed. "If you think I'm going back out there tonight, you're crazy!"

Healy threw a paternal arm around Larry's still-quivering shoulders: "You'll do fine," he smiled.

Larry had the look of a trapped animal as Healy ushered him into his dressing room. Healy stepped back and regarded him in the classic Healy pose of contemplation: elbow resting on palm, mouth cupped with a half-open fist. He raised an eyebrow and took the measure of Larry's unhappiness.

"Hold that look — it's great," he told Larry. "That frown almost makes you look old enough to vote."

Larry doubled up with laughter. All of a sudden, the sheer nuttiness of the day hit him like a sandbag from the rafters. If this Healy maniac wanted to control Larry's life for awhile, why not? He didn't have any other plans.

"All right, what do you want me to do?" said Larry.

He finished the show that night. And by the time he got home to Mabel, he was walking with the swagger of the Conquering Hero.

Mabel was delighted: "This could be the break you've been waiting for, Larry."

By this time, she had been feeling a little guilty about pulling Larry off the Canadian Circuit. And now she was willing to leave the Haney Sisters behind and follow her husband whenever the show was ready to close in Chicago.

Larry spent all day Thursday in rehearsal with Healy and Shemp and was ready to do the whole show Thursday night.

Mabel saw it Friday night with some misgivings. She was ready to go along with it, but that didn't mean she had to agree with it. She often had second thoughts about Larry's acts in those days. It was the only thing I've ever seen them argue about.

She winced when the weight of the Healy sadism was first brought to bear on her poor husband. But the approval of the audience reassured her a bit. And she was impressed by how big, how *spectacular* the whole production was. The sets were lavish, and there must have been more than a hundred people in the cast.

Shemp shot out of town the next day to join Jack Waldron in New York. Larry had another two weeks to get comfortable with his role on his then-home turf of Chicago. But on April 5, Jolson's contract was up, the show closed, and it was time to hit the road.

The Shuberts, heartened by the show's success in the nation's "Second City," were prepared to push it vigorously on the road. On April 8, it opened in Pittsburgh. And on April 29, it was in Detroit, where Larry was starting to get some attention in the press as Healy's "bum."

Seeing yourself characterized in the news as a "bum" takes some getting used to. But Larry decided he kind of liked it. It was as good a description as any of the role he'd been hired to play.

By mid-summer, though, Mabel had a different role for the neophyte stooge: expectant father. Mabel was pregnant with their first child.

In the days before Disneyland, Atlantic City was "America's playground." Its boardwalk was the biggest in the world, an extravaganza of rides, arcades and showmanship. Its beaches were so packed with people that you couldn't see the sand. When Mabel was a little girl, it was her vision of Heaven. She'd be furious when a weekend or vacation was over, and it was time to go back to gray, old Philadelphia. She promised herself that when she grew up, she was going to live in Atlantic City. Her children would never have to tear themselves away from the pleasures of the shore just to go home. They'd already be home.

Now that she was actually going to have a child, it was time to satisfy the willful girl of her past. When *A Night in Spain* finally disbanded, Larry and Mabel headed straight for Atlantic City. The Haneys and the Feinbergs were delighted: the fabled resort town was a lot closer to Philadelphia than Chicago had been.

The beach at Atlantic City with Steel Pier in the background.
(from the collection of the Free Library of Philadelphia: Arthur Soll, Research Photographer)

Everything seemed to work in their favor. The summer season was over, and places to live were cheap and abundant. Mabel's brother, Tom, owned a thriving taxi business in town. He enjoyed the prospect of becoming an uncle and eagerly helped them get settled, doting over Mabel as if she were a princess. Employment was no problem. There were plenty of clubs, even in the off-season, that were looking for an engaging, young emcee to fill their nights with song and mirth. Atlantic City was just far enough removed from the world of the Shuberts that clubs could get away with billing Larry as the *star* of *A Night In Spain*. No one was ever the wiser.

In no time, the Fines had built a tranquil nest, far from the rigors of the road. The holiday season had never seemed more cheerful. And on the morning of February 9, 1929, Phyllis Fine was born.

Larry was overwhelmed with joy. The club date he had to play that night wound up to be more of a party than a show. Many a cigar was handed out, and many a *mazel tov* collected.

It's a Jewish tradition to name the newborn child in honor of a departed relative. By invoking the past, we give it new life. And Mother was pleased that Larry and Mabel had named their firstborn after our brother Philip. Phyllis, God willing, would be blessed with the long life Philip never had.

Among the well-wishers who phoned in the weeks that followed were Ted and Betty Healy. Ted, as usual, had more than pleasantries up his sleeve: he had a proposal. The Shuberts were mounting a new revue, another "international" affair, to be called *A Night In Venice*. But this time, Healy didn't just want one stooge; he wanted to surround himself with stooges. Shemp Howard was going to be in the show, his new act hadn't worked out so well, and Moe, Shemp's brother, was going to join them. Healy wanted Larry, too; three stooges.

Larry was reluctant to leave his new family even for the allure of Broadway, but Mabel talked him into it. She had wanted to take a trip to Philadelphia, to show their daughter off to the hometown crowd.

So Larry went to New York while Mabel and Phyllis stayed with Mother, Lyla and me. It was a full house again, and Mother was the happiest she'd been in years. Phyllis's Aunt Lyla was eight at the time and was a devoted babysitter for her living doll of a niece.

We went out almost every night, and I was the chauffeur,

ferrying my happy brood from relative to relative. One night, as we were passing the Liberty Bell, Mabel burst into giggles.

"Philadelphia sure is a great vacation spot," she said. "When you live in Atlantic City."

HAIR OF THE STOOGE ~~~~~~~~~~ *1929*

By the end of March, rehearsals for *A Night In Venice* had assumed an air of urgency. It was due to begin a trial run in Newark the day after April Fools' Day. Everywhere there were last-minute details to attend to, tiny touches of magic that could spell success or doom for the lavish show. So when Larry dashed into rehearsal a half-hour late one day, he found himself face to face with a furious Jake Shubert.

Although the program would bill *A Night In Venice* as a production of the "Messrs. Shubert," the show was clearly Jake's baby — rich in the fast-paced slapstick and countless scantily-clad girls that were Jake's trademarks. Lee, however, was President of the Shubert Theatrical Corporation. And the way he underscored that fact to his surly brother, with whom he never spoke but through intermediaries, was to deny Jake full production credits.

"Where the hell do you think you're going?" Jake howled to Larry.

"Dressing room, sir. To comb my hair," said Larry. He had overslept, taken a quick shower, thrown on his clothes and raced out the door. His hair was a frazzled mess.

"You get on that stage, *right now,* or I make you *eat* your hair!"

Larry, Moe, and Shemp from *Shivering Sherlocks* (1948).
(Photo by Gereghty, from the collection of Steve Cox)

Larry scrambled up on the stage, but Jake was right on his tail. The esteemed Mr. Shubert wasn't quite through with our hero.

"Look at me!" he barked.

White of countenance and weak of knee, Larry turned to face the part-owner of nearly half the theaters of consequence in America.

Jake slammed two pudgy paws on the sides of Larry's head and violently rubbed his hair. "There," said Jake, stepping back to inspect his handiwork. "Now you look like a stooge! I don't wanna see your hair combed again — ever!"

"You know, I hate to admit it," Healy later told Larry, "but I think ole Jake was right for once. You look great with your hair all frizzed up like that."

Larry's new style fit right in with the act. Shemp's long, stringy hair looked like it had been cut every six months or so with a jackknife. While Moe Howard had apparently discovered the value of a pair of scissors, his hairstylist was a bowl. But Shemp and Moe had been working with Healy, off and on, for the better part of a decade, and Larry was still catching up.

Moe once told me how the whole idea of Healy stooges had come about.

Moe and Shemp were ambling down a Brooklyn street in 1922, when they were stopped short by a familiar name emblazoned across a theater marquee: "Ted and Betty Healy." The Howards had heard through the grapevine that their old childhood chum, Lee Nash, had gotten married and changed his name to "Ted Healy." This had to be the same guy, doing an act with his wife. They decided to catch the show and maybe heckle the old boy a bit.

Healy recognized the noisy pair in the front row right away and invited them up onstage as "volunteers from the audience." Part of Healy's act involved a trapeze bit, but his acrobats had just quit the day before. So he told Moe and Shemp to strip to their long johns, had the trapezes lowered and ordered them on. Back up to the rafters went the trapezes, this time with the puzzled Howards. And there they remained for the rest of the show. Shemp was scared of heights and carried on like a banshee between acts, but the audience had a great time.

After that, they worked out other bits, and Healy had them back the next night — and the next, and the next. Years rolled by. Sometimes, one or the other of the Howards would leave to do another act or try another business. Moe had been busily failing at real estate during the run of *A Night In Spain*. But they kept coming back to Healy.

In a sense, Healy had never released them from those trapezes, high above the stage. Now Larry, with his new hairstyle, was up there with them.

A NIGHT IN VENICE ~~~~~~~~~~ *1929*

Most musicals, in those days, had a mere shadow of a story-line, more of a premise than a plot, on which to string their varied scenes. *A Night In Venice* concerned two hapless lovers who pose as daring pilots in the Lindbergh mold to win the hearts of two winsome showgirls. Word leaks out that they've flown to Europe — crossed the Atlantic — and landed in Venice. The girls book passage to meet them, and when they arrive in the Italian city of twisting waterways and drifting gondolas, a gala party is being given in honor of the two con artists. After much merriment, scenes and scenes of it, the girls discover the elaborate hoax. But by this time, everyone is having too good a time to care.

Ted Healy & the Dodge Twins, Beth and Betty, in *A Night in Venice*
(Billy Rose Theatre Collection of the New York Public Library)

That may not look like much in cold type, but onstage it was dazzling. The great Busby Berkeley, later to become the King of MGM musicals, did the monumental staging. Newark was floored, unanimously praising it in the press: "a gorgeous production," "opulent in scenic and sartorial display." The Shuberts were pleased and readied a spot for it to open on Broadway: Tuesday night, May 21, at the Shubert Theater.

There's something about a Broadway opening that humbles everyone who stares into its fearsome visage. It gathers over the horizon like a dark storm over choice farmland. And no one knows whether it'll thunder into nourishing rain or turn deathly still, dropping a tornado on the farmhouse. A good opening can fully employ more than a hundred talented people for a year or more; a bad one can send the same crew scurrying for cover. Millions of dollars can hang in the balance. How could even a week at the Palace compete with that for high stakes on the stage?

Larry experienced it in the form of acid indigestion.

Healy had the most malleable face I've ever seen, and he scrunched it up in imitation of a prune when he saw Larry's sodium bicarb. "There's only one cure for what you got," he told him. "Footlights! Footlights and an audience!"

It was the Dr. Theodore C. Healy Cure, patent applied for, and it worked wonders. As soon as Larry hit the boards, he was more than his old self. They all gave it everything they had, and the applause was clearly more thunder than tornado. It looked like a hit.

The cast spent nearly an hour, after final curtain, genuinely enjoying themselves: hugging each other, signing autographs with a flourish, visiting with old friends who had timidly walked backstage....

But all too soon, it was time for that dread Broadway phenomenon, the "Opening Night Cast Party."

So after a breather, the cast jammed itself into someone's apartment, a cell with white walls, to await the early editions of the morning papers. Forced gaiety etched the illusion of a party through the fog of boredom and stress.

Finally the *Times* arrived, and its review saved the day. It wasn't just a good review; it was a rave. Amongst the heroes of the moment were none other than Ted Healy and his unkempt bums!

Here's how it began:

> Early in the second half of *A Night In Venice,* which thumped into view at the Shubert last evening, Ted Healy, his band and his gang staged a knockabout skit concerning a substitute act from Atlantic City. Healy, whom you will remember as the comedian with the shiny frontal bald spot, is leading his jazz band while three of the frowsiest numskulls ever assembled are trying to put over, with the familiar flourishes of show business, a ballad about that dress that Nellie wore. It is, you will remember, innocuous enough until the most vocal and disreputable of the trio insists upon injecting, between bars, two thick-witted claps of the hand and two "Hey, hey's" — denoting rising enthusiasm. Then it is that the scuffle begins, shirt fronts are torn, feet are stamped on, and the singer is savagely tackled around the neck.

The reviewer went on to call the skit a "masterpiece of slapstick comedy, and the best number in the new Summer carnival."

The cast exploded in cheers.

"Come on with me, boys," said Healy to Larry and the Howards, "we've gotta show this to my dear, old Aunt Matilda."

TED HEALY AND HIS THREE SOUTHERN GENTLEMEN 〰〰〰〰〰 1929

A Night in Venice continued its merry run on the road, but it was blindly set on a collision course with grim forces of history.

For months, eccentric economists had been claiming that stock market prices were unrealistically inflated, that sooner or later, the market was going to have to "bottom out." "Alarmist" was the word for those guys. But on Black Thursday, October 24, they seemed to be, if anything, a little optimistic. The market plummeted out of sight, causing millions of dollars to literally vanish overnight and several captains of capitalism to dive out of skyscrapers into the oblivion below.

The Shuberts had a flurry of shows set to open in New York and were in no mood for further risk-taking. They cast a frugal eye to the road and saw *A Night in Venice,* an expensive show that had to do pretty well just to stay afloat. The Shuberts decided to pull the plug.

But Ted Healy had been one of vaudeville's brightest stars before joining the Shuberts to try his hand at musical comedy. And vaudeville was in trouble: the movies, musicals and radio were conspiring to steal its best talent. Healy and the gang were snapped up by the prestigious Marcus Loew Circuit in an instant.

"It's hard to remember just when *A Night in Venice* folded," Larry told me later. "One night, we were slapping each other around in a musical comedy, and the next, we were doing the same act as 'Ted Healy And His Three Southern Gentlemen.' We didn't skip a beat."

Ted Healy was the prodigal son come home to the vaude stage that had first given him fame. And with him was a gang of stooges at once more raffish and more polished than ever.

They took the name for their act from this routine:

> Ted: "Who are you gentlemen?"
> Stooges: "We're from the South."
> Ted: "From the South, eh? Ever hear of Abraham Lincoln?"
> Moe: "Glad to meet you, Mr. Lincoln."
> Larry: "Real pleasure."
> Shemp: "Regards to Mrs. Lincoln."
> Ted gets caught up in a flurry of handshakes, then stops short in a pause pregnant with exasperation and lets loose with his dread triple slap.

Larry and the Howards carried their share of the comic load and then some. But it was Healy who drew the fans. It was his rubbery face that could assume any character he pleased.

But the Shubert years had added an extra twist to the Healy *schtick:* a certain Broadway saltiness of speech that may have worked with Jake's naughty musicals but was anathema to the family fun of vaudeville.

Above all else, vaudeville was wholesome. Some of you older youngsters will recall the *Ed Sullivan Show* in the Fifties:

animal acts, clowns, singers, bits of musicals, comics, all together in a happy spectacle. That was vaudeville, and nothing was more vaude than their refusal to show Elvis' twisting pelvis as he sang *Hound Dog.*

It was probably this very innocence that allowed vaudeville to survive as long as it did. As the Depression deepened, things that had been disdained as old-fashioned were suddenly being cheered as reassuringly familiar.

Healy, on the other hand, was not out to "reassure" anyone. His soul was of the Jazz Age: for him, it would always be one in the morning in his favorite speakeasy on Broadway in 1929.

Once upon a time, Ted was travelling with three gentlemen of the South on the road that Loew built. They were in a show, and a wonderful show it was. Acrobats, there were — and singers, and comics, and bears.

One of the bears, the wee tiniest one, left a bear dropping onstage just as our Ted made his entrance so grand.

"The bear! The bear! We want the bear!" yelled the well-oiled crowd.

Our Ted knocked back his fedora and rubbed his chin, to ponder the crowd.

"Well, if that's the kind of crap you want," he said, "I'll give it to ya, myself!"

The crowd loved it; the management fired him — him and his "gentlemen."

Larry was elated. The very next day, he was back in Atlantic City, feeding the baby and decorating the Christmas tree.

Moe Howard called that night to make sure that Larry was okay. They had almost been ready to phone him in as a "missing person," he had left so fast.

"You coming back to the act?" Moe asked. "Ted just landed a run on the Keith Circuit."

"When does it start?"

"Don't worry: not till after the holidays," said Moe. "And it includes the Palace! We're gonna play the Palace, Larry!"

Larry turned and stared at Mabel and Phyllis. "The Palace," he informed them.

Phyllis burbled something that Larry could have sworn

sounded just like, "Take it!"

He turned back to the phone: "Count me in."

THE PALACE 〰〰〰〰〰〰〰〰〰〰〰 1930

In the days before neon, Broadway was literally the Great White Way. Little white electric bulbs marked the marquees, and marquees were everywhere. Broadway at night, between 38th and 48th Streets, was a radiant boulevard fallen from Heaven and still glowing with all its might.

Near the North Pole of this magic were three buildings crammed into the space between 47th Street and Seventh Avenue. At Broadway and Seventh was a Whelen's Drugstore; at 47th Street was a squat office building. Sandwiched between them was a thin, windowless structure, totally nondescript but for a modest marquee which bore this legend: The Palace Theater.

At the entrance of this unimposing frame was "the beach." It would have looked just like a sidewalk to you and me, and that's exactly what it was. But it was "the beach" to the unemployed vaudevilleans who gathered there, night and day. It was there that they plotted the ways they would build the ships that could sail the waves of the tumultuous applause inside. And it was there that they just goofed off and traded gossip.

The big news just now was that one of their own, a sad-faced xylophonist named Fred Sanborn that even the "beach" gang hadn't paid much attention to, had been snapped up by the great Ted Healy and was — get this — *headlining* with Healy and his assorted misfits for the last week in February.

With his bushy, black eyebrows and his long, dour face, Fred Sanborn looked like Groucho Marx with a hangover, a perfect supplement for Healy's gallery of rogues. Now there were four of them, each as odd as the other.

"Mark my words," warned Shemp, "one of these days, it'll be 'Ted Healy and the U.S. Army'."

Fred Sanborn had mixed feelings about all of this and spent a lot of time backstage with Larry, lamenting the absence of his xylophone. He wanted to make it as a musician and didn't want to be typecast as a "Healyite."

FRED SANBORN

Fred Sanborn's logo when he worked as a solo act.

At first, Larry lent a sympathetic ear to Freddie's endless *kvetching*. Larry after all, still thought of himself as a violinist. But enough was enough. This wasn't Podunck, Indiana; they were finally set to play the Palace — the real one, the one in New York, the hottest venue in vaudeville. Not only that, they were "next-to-closing," the most venerated spot on the bill.

An evening at the Palace consisted of about nine acts, set in a traditional order. Each spot on the bill, in fact, had its own legacy, its own heroes, its own unique aesthetic.

The program usually began with a "dumb act" — silent, not stupid, though some claimed it was both. It was an animal act, say, or a clown act that required full stage. Latecomers, a staple of the New York crowd, could feel free to seat themselves in the middle of the act without sitting on a punch line.

From then on, the bill would alternate between acts that worked on "one," before the first backdrop, and those that needed full stage.

"Closing intermission," the last act before intermission, and usually the fifth act of the evening, was one of two "headlining" positions. Most vaude houses were content with one headliner per program. The Palace often had two, and the headliner that worked full stage would play "closing intermission."

The show would resume with an act on "one," followed by a full stage act, perhaps a one-act play. "Next-to-closing" was next. In every other vaude house, the "next-to-closing" act was where the headliner went. At the Palace, it was where the headliner that could work on "one" went.

"Closing" was one of two things: another "dumb act" like the opening, or a whirlwind grand finale combining all the evening's acts.

Ted Healy and his slovenly quartet were to comprise the sole headlining act that cold, last week in February: next-to-closing, top o' the world.

(l. to r.) Larry, Moe, Ted Healy, Shemp, and Fred Sanborn in a postcard advertising Chicago's Hotel McCormick's "Special Rates to the Profession."
(from the collection of Joe Wallison)

TED HEALY AND HIS RACKETEERS ～～～ 1930

"Tell ya the truth, I wasn't too crazy about that 'Racketeers' bit on our posters, but I went along with it." It was E.F. Albee, manager of both the Keith Circuit and the Palace wagging his finger at Ted Healy's face. But it was Healy's stooges, ever at his side, who did the squirming.

"I want you to know," Albee went on, "that I won't tolerate any cussing on my stage. You don't say, 'God damn.' You don't say, 'devil.' You don't say, 'hell.' You don't say, 'spit.' You don't say, 'cockroach.' Get my drift?"

Healy and the boys got it, in spades. There's something ugly about a guy who truly thinks a word is "dirty" and pronounces it anyway. Healy could have said all those words as casually as a conductor announcing the presence of "Wilkes-Barre." But Healy half-expected green spit to ooze down the corners of Mr. Albee's mouth during his recitation of the word, "cockroach." Albee genuinely loathed those words, and it showed.

Mr. Albee rarely felt the need to spell these things out: his "do"s and "don't"s were common knowledge in vaude circles. But there was a lot riding on this show for all concerned. New York was Healy's home turf, and it seemed as if the whole city had been holding its breath to witness the Disreputable One's takeover of the Palace. Albee was willing to pay for a good draw — the word on "the beach" was that Healy was getting $6,000 for the week's engagement. But no one wanted a rerun of the Loew fiasco.

Speaking of money, I should point out that Albee, like the Shuberts and the Loew people before him, never paid Healy's stooges a cent. They paid Healy for the whole act and left it to him to divide the spoils. The magnanimous Mr. Healy paid each of his cohorts $100 a week.

That may sound a bit scrimpy compared to the soaring rumors of Healy's earnings. But $100 was a substantial weekly pay in those days. And Healy — for whatever reason — was perpetually broke, no matter what he made. He was always in the middle of some Rube Goldberg scheme to avoid his creditors. You could have given him a million dollars, and it would have been like throwing it out the window. He'd still be living one step ahead of the landlord.

In any event, they all more than earned their keep. Healy and his Racketeers were a smash.

"Tell ya what I'm gonna do," beamed Mr. Albee, backstage one night. "I'm gonna do what I used to say I'd never do, not for anyone: I'm gonna hold you over for another week."

Healy leaned forward: "As headliners."

"As headliners, of course!" said Albee. "Unfortunately,

you'll have to share the honors with another act next week, but..."

"We'll be next-to-closing," Healy shot back.

"We were hoping you'd consider closing intermission. You must remember that a second week in a row here is almost unprecedented."

"Don't get me wrong, Mr. Albee," said Healy. "I'm flattered by your offer. And my boys, here, are flattered; aren't you, boys?"

Healy's wide-eyed boys were very flattered, indeed. Shemp glared a silent warning to Healy not to blow it.

"But it's really out of my hands," Healy went on. "A simple extension of the contract would be one thing, but such a wholesale revision of the contract....Well, you really have to speak to my agent."

The negotiations between Albee and Healy's agent were still going on the next day, far too long for comfort. Larry and Moe were getting nervous: they desperately wanted to extend their run. Freddie was sanguine, as usual, but no one noticed. Shemp was furious, and that made even Healy nervous.

As far as Healy was concerned, Shemp was still the stooge *par excellence.* If a skit required a single stooge, Shemp was the one Healy picked. If a skit required one of the bunch to take the lead and raise the act to greater rowdiness, Shemp got the nod. It was Shemp who the *New York Times* had deemed the "most disreputable of the trio" in the Shubert days. And it was Shemp who Healy always referred to as "irreplaceable."

So it was with great relief that Healy and his horde greeted the news that Healy's gambit had worked. A settlement had been reached, and they were to do the second week.

For their extended engagement, they shared the headline with Henry Santrey's "Soldiers of Fortune," a 17-man orchestra which spiced its tunes with singing and dancing. Healy and his unsavory brigade went on at closing intermission, the second headliner's spot, but intermission didn't finish their act. They wove themselves all over the second half as well, performing little skits between acts like lunatic emcees. In all, they filled 45 minutes of each show.

The *New York Times,* sizing up the evening's entertainment, was forced "to conclude that Mr. Healy and the boys are what matter. There has been no more amusing act than theirs at the Palace in a vast parcel of Sunday afternoons."

A mere mention by the *Times* was a high honor for a vaudeville act, even a Palace one. The *Times* was generally pleased to leave the day-to-day vaude stage to *Variety* and its ilk, in favor of musical comedy and the "legit stage." Only the most newsworthy of vaude happenings were deemed "fit to print."

So eyebrows were raised as the *Times* reviewer went on and on with the enthusiasm of a true believer:

> The battered Healy hat...still marches with its owner at the head of such a band of unkempt ruffians and gladiators as could never have paraded a stage before ....Sometimes it is Mr. Healy alone (Theodore Z. Healy, to you, when he wears a silk hat); generally it is Mr. Healy, accompanied by his lieutenants Shemp and Moe Howard, and the gang in a deal of hilarious horseplay. It is rough and hardy sport, but unendingly funny, whether the boys are burlesquing "Street Scene" or Mr. Healy is swaggering about in a leopard skin. His followers are all a little balmy and their king does everything wrong. You can count on that.

In a meeting of Hollywood's Fox Studio, the Healy name found itself placed on a crowded agenda. The *Times* review was passed around to nods of assent. They had just the movie for an act like that. It was the one being written by a cartoonist — a vaude cartoonist, at that, with a hit song to his credit. They'd be perfect.

A phone call was placed to Healy's agent in New York.

Albee was so impressed by the *Times* review that he invited Healy and the boys back for a totally unprecedented third week.

"As headliners?" Healy asked with the relentless predictability of a clock.

"I can't do that, Ted," moaned Albee. "We're the Keepers of a Flame, here, and I have to look to tradition. If I kept you on as a headliner for three weeks straight, we wouldn't be vaudeville. We wouldn't be the Palace."

"No deal," said Healy.

"Listen: we'll bill you as an 'Extra Added Attraction.' You wouldn't be headliners, but we'd pull out all the stops. We need you, Ted. Vaudeville needs you."

"Stuff it up your tradition," said Healy, as he walked out the backstage door.

NEW DIRECTIONS 〰〰〰〰〰〰〰〰 1930

Back home in Philadelphia, little Lyla was chirping happily into the phone. She held the handset to her ear with both hands as if it were a teddy bear, and her expression flipped freely from rapt attention to hysterical laughter to wide-eyed wonder.

It was easy to tell who was on the other end of the line. "It's our brother, the movie star," Lyla squealed as she handed me the phone. "Rube Goldberg is writing a movie for him."

"Movie star? Rube Goldberg?" I shook my head. Lyla adored Larry. To her, he was the King of Vaudeville, the best violinist in the world and — when he came home to Philadelphia from his glamorous adventures — her surrogate Daddy. All of these fancies were based on kernels of truth. But movie star? That was a new one.

"Well, now you've done it," I told Larry. "Lyla's gone nuts."

"Lyla's not nuts," said Larry. "It's Hollywood that's nuts. Healy signed to do a movie for Fox, and we're all gonna be in it. Even Freddie's in on it."

"So how does Rube Goldberg figure in? Lyla said..."

"...he's writing it. Yeah, it's true, Moe. It's gonna be a smash.

I must have looked pretty surprised, because Lyla was rolling on the floor, punctuating her laughter with bursts of: "I told ya, Moe! I told ya!"

Rube Goldberg was easily one of America's most popular cartoonists, the guy who put the "funny" in the "funny papers." One of my earliest memories is of Dad reading me Goldberg's *Foolish Questions* strip in the paper when he came home from work. Here's an example:

"Son, are you smoking that pipe again?"
"No, Dad, this is a portable kitchenette, and I'm frying a smelt for dinner."

I learned how to read by the light of his strip. When I had gotten good at it, he started drawing, *I'm The Guy,* one of my favorites. Goldberg even wrote a song called *I'm The Guy,* with Bert Grant, and it became a real hit around our Gramophone. It was a lot like the strip:

"I'm the guy that put the salt in the ocean,
I'm the guy that put the bones in fish.
I'm the guy that's five five high
I'll always live, I'll never die —
I'm the guy that put the wishbone in the wish.

I'm the guy that put the skin on bananas,
I'm the guy that put the leaves on trees.
What's that, who am I?
Why don't you know, I'm the guy —
I'm the guy that put the holes in Switzer cheese."

In those days, cartoonists didn't have to draw the same strip every day. One day, Goldberg would do a *Foolish Question;* the next day, he'd do an *I'm The Guy.* Then he might do *Boob McNutt* for two days straight. You never knew. The important thing was that it was a Goldberg, which meant that it was going to be good.

By the time I was ten or so, he was throwing in an occasional *The Inventions of Professor Butts*: the strip that was to assure his eternal fame. The Professor's "simple appliances" were zany satires of Goldberg's youthful training as a mechanical engineer. Rockets shot off to the moon; dogs kicked over hat racks in fright; igloos melted; stenographers picked up umbrellas; dictators collapsed — all to serve as parts of a chain of events that would "effortlessly" perform a simple task, placing a postage stamp on an envelope, for example.

Even Healy was excited about having Rube Goldberg as his writer, and he was especially pleased about doing a movie. Everyone was talking about the "death of vaudeville," and how it was time to get into pictures. Well, now he was doing it.

He was going to hit Hollywood with the largest and weirdest collection of stooges ever. Even all the wives and kids were coming. Larry and Mabel saw it as a chance to take a summer vacation in sunny California while making a shrewd career move. That was fine with Healy: it made his royal retinue even bigger.

"Mabel's been singing, *California, Here I Come,* all day long Larry told me. "She puts my Jolson imitation to shame."

All of Healy's stooges' wives were exceptionally beautiful, and it wouldn't surprise me if he had planned to introduce them all as his girlfriends.

A few days later, a train pulled out of Grand Central Station in Manhattan, aimed at Los Angeles. In it were: Ted and Betty Healy, Larry and Mabel Fine, Moe and Helen Howard, Shemp and Babe Howard, and Freddie Sanborn, ever the loner.

It was a most congenial crossing of the continent, a four-day party against an ever-changing backdrop of mountains, plains, buttes, forests and deserts. Mabel and Betty, the old vaude hands, worked out a few duets to gladden the way through the relentless plains. But Mabel formed her greatest alliance with the Howards, Helen and Babe.

Helen was the quiet one with the grace of an aristocrat. The great Houdini was her Cousin Harry. Babe was the extrovert, round-faced as the "smile button" of the 1960s surrounded by the blond curls of a vamp.

They were like schoolgirls at a slumber party, laughing the nights away.

SOUP TO NUTS ~~~~~~~~~~~~~1930

The first thing Ted Healy and his Transcontinental Merry-Makers did upon arriving in Hollywood was check into a hotel and go to bed early. None of the fabled pleasures of America's Dream Factory could compare with sleeping in a bed that wasn't loudly clanging back and forth through the long night. And besides, they had work to do.

The next morning, a well-rested quintet appeared at the administration building on the main Fox lot on Western Avenue.

The receptionist had been expecting them: "Don't tell me: let me guess. You're Ted Healy and his Racketeers, right? Just leave your machine guns by the door and have a seat. Mr. Stoloff will be right over."

Healy had hardly started flirting with his pretty greeter when Ben Stoloff burst through the door. Stoloff was a ruggedly handsome guy, dressed in the "California Casual" style: sports shirt, white slacks and tennis shoes. He stuck his cigar into his bemused half-smile and extended his hand to Healy.

"Ted Healy, I presume," said Stoloff, as he pumped Healy's hand.

"Let me guess," said Healy, with a wink to receptionist. "You're the director."

"You're darned right, and I expect great things from you in this picture..."

"Wait a minute," said Shemp. "That guy's an imposter! I'm Ted Healy!"

"Don't listen to that jerk," said Moe. "I'm Ted Healy!"

"We're expecting great things from all you boys," Stoloff corrected himself as he led them to his office.

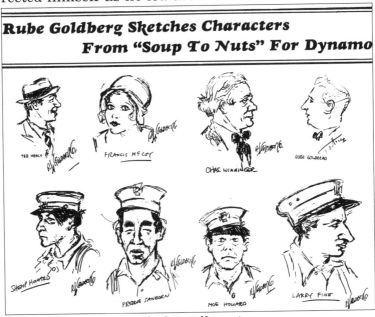

Rube Goldberg Sketches Characters From "Soup To Nuts" For Dynamo

Rube Goldberg's caricatures of the *Soup to Nuts* cast.
(from the collection of Greg & Jeff Lenburg)

The movie was to be called *Soup To Nuts,* as in a smorgasbord of slapstick. What the Fox people had in mind was an extravagant toast to the old Keystone two-reelers, with a heavy dose of romantic *schmaltz* to bring it all up-to-date.

Healy was to play the romantic lead, a role he considered right up his alley. Larry and the boys were to supply the

"Keystone" touch as comic extras: firemen in some scenes, Mexican revolutionaries in others — but always possessed by the spirit of the Keystone Kops.

"When do I see a script?" Healy wanted to know. "All I've seen so far is the storyline."

Ben Stoloff settled into his cocky half-smile. "As soon as *I* do," he said. "We've got Mr. Goldberg locked in one of our trailers with one of our boys, Howard Green. We expect a final revision anytime now. In the meantime, you might look this over. It's what we'll be shooting the day after tomorrow."

Stoloff pushed a stack of paper across his desk toward Healy.

"Right now, though," said Stoloff, "we've gotta get you boys fitted for costumes."

To Larry, the most impressive — and unexpected — part of movie-making was all the time you spent just goofing off while the crew set up the next scene. Larry and the boys weren't even in most of the scenes, so they wound up playing with their families at the beach or losing at the racetrack for days at a time. Even when they were filming, most of their time was devoted to playing cards or hanging out at the studio commissary, meeting celebrities.

All of the boys, of course, had long since gotten over the novelty of meeting and working with the biggest stars of the vaudeville stage. But these people were movie stars! And Larry, at least, found himself acting like a starstuck kid who had somehow slipped past security and found himself at the heart of the studio.

Midway through the production, he even got to meet the jug-eared genius of the comics whose name had lured them all to Fox in the first place.

Rube Goldberg had finally finished the last scenes of the script and was free to join in the cast's bored merriment. He sat around in a canvas chair, drew pencil sketches of the actors, traded quips and consumed cigars in the tranquil Hollywood summer sun.

When he got back to New York, Goldberg would dismiss the entire project as a bitter experience that had shaved years from his life. But just between you and me, even the frantically busy Rube Goldberg had his shot at a little peace and relaxation. Everyone walked away from the project with a good remembrance or more.

It's a pity that the Fox studio heads and the general public didn't have the same good feeling about the finished *Soup To Nuts*. The Fox executives were disappointed and sent the film out to "one night stand" movie houses. The critics smelled blood and moved in for the kill.

Here's what *Variety* had to say:

> Skeleton of the story as may be seen through this abortive comedy looks to be funny. The cast is full of comedians but they are all straight men excepting Ted Healy's stooges, and the stooges are a Mexican army of revolutionaries for their 'funniest' moment in the old Keystone style. Other Keystoners are a fire house and truck, and a fire and more fire.
>
> Ted Healy and Charles Winniger are turned into a couple of straight men in what was intended for a comedy picture. Winniger does play his trombone when he's supposedly sober and soused, and not too comically either time. Not only is Healy, a comedian whom the New York Palace pays $6,000 a week for headlining in that ace vaude house, made a straight man, but he is turned into a flip romantic juvenile with a girl as unfunny as he is here, hanging onto his neck all the while. The rest, in people and action, goes along with that.
>
> It's Rube Goldberg's first written scenario, and a pity that that famous cartoonist's pen must have been so butchered.

Ted Healy was on a platform, preparing to board a train for New York when he heard a disquieting bit of gossip: the Fox people felt that Healy's four Racketeers were the best part of the movie and had decided to sign them up — without Healy.

To say that it didn't set well with Healy is an understatement. Healy was the star; Healy was the Big Name that had brought these guys to Hollywood in the first place. He was not about to let them upstage him.

The next day, he stormed into Winfield Sheehan's office: Sheehan was not only Fox's head of production, he was one of Healy's biggest fans — the perfect man to see.

"Listen, Winnie," said Healy, "let's talk one Irishman to another. Those guys are mine. I invented them. You take them without me, you cut out my heart. Wanna cut out my heart?"

Mr. Sheehan wanted nothing of the sort. He simply wanted a cheap act: he knew that the Healyites were making $100 apiece for each week of the shoot out of Healy's $1,250 a week. He was prepared to pay that, but he didn't want Healy's animosity.

"Keep your heart," he assured Healy. "Keep your boys — we don't have a contract."

"You're a man for the ages," said Healy, with a great sigh. "There's only one more thing: don't tell the boys about all this. Tell 'em you ran out of money or something. They're neophytes. They don't know."

Mr. Sheehan shrugged his shoulders: "I'll do what I can."

But the Hollywood grapevine is fast and furious. The boys were due to sign their contract the next day, and there was no shortage of old Hollywood hands to hint at why the signing was being put off, rethought, cancelled.

Larry was confused, but the Howards were furious. Healy was, after all, their boyhood chum, and he had betrayed them. "We've got to hit the road on our own," Shemp insisted. "This time he's gone too far!"

"Maybe it wasn't his fault," Larry suggested.

Shemp rolled his eyes: "You with us or what?"

Larry was forever the easy mark. If he'd been with Healy, he might have seen Healy's point of view. But he was with the Howards. Freddie Sanborn wasn't with anyone. When the contract fell through, he rushed back to his xylophone.

"I'm with you," said Larry.

They sent the girls home, and hustled up an engagement at Hollywood's Paramount Theater.

"Who's afraid of the big, bad Healy?" Larry liked to ask.

They all were. But they were willing to give freedom a shot.

A POKE IN THE EYES ~~~~~~~~~~~~ *1930*

Dictionaries differ on the precise nature of a "stooge." Random House defines the term as "an entertainer who feeds lines to the main comedian and usually serves as the butt of his jokes." Webster's gives more of a historical overview: "originally, in the theater, a paid heckler who harassed the comedian on the stage from a seat in the audience." The new

American Heritage dictionary ignores the theatrical connotation and says simply: "one who allows himself to be used for another's profit."

Larry and the Howards would have found merit in all three of these definitions. And they all suggest the depth of the dilemma that the hapless Healyites now found themselves in. To be a stooge was to be in a subordinate position relative to a commanding boss of some sort. Now they were like three moons without a planet, three *bar mitzvah* boys without a rabbi. They were three stooges without a top banana.

Larry started to suggest that they do a revival of *At The Crossroads*, his old Haney Sisters and Fine act. But the notion was soundly hooted down before he could get out his violin or even finish his sentence.

Their best shot was to rework the Healy act. They could use the Paramount's emcee to set up the various comic situations. But one of the stooges was going to have to be the one to mete out the slaps, yanks, pokes, punches and kicks that got them their biggest laughs.

Shemp had always been the head stooge: he was Moe's big brother, and Healy considered him the best comedian of the bunch. But it was Moe who could scrunch up his mouth and chin like a bulldog watching a mailman. All three of them could look disreputable enough; Moe, though, could look downright mean. So Moe was elected chief tormentor. Larry wasn't even considered: he looked about as vicious as chicken soup.

The boys plunged into rehearsal with a vengeance, determined to prove that they could make it without their mentor. By the day of their opening at the Hollywood Paramount, they were satisfied with their revamped act and had nothing left to tackle but their nervousness.

A friendly game of cards seemed just the cure for their gathering stage fright. Their favorite game was an East European import called *klabyash*. It was played with two decks, using only the numbered cards from ace to nine. The idea was to make "nines": if you put a six down, the other guy could slap down a three and take them in. The one that was left with the most cards in his hand lost.

I must have watched them dozens of times, but I could never get the hang of the game. What I remember most vividly was all the screaming and cursing that always seemed to dominate the proceedings. You'd think they were playing for blood.

The first few times I saw them play, I thought, "Well, this is it. They're gonna dissolve the act and never speak to each other again."

But when they got through playing, they'd go off arm in arm like the good buddies they were. To the Howards, Larry was what we call *mishpocheh*: one of the family. They could call each other the worst names in the world, but nothing ever cut into their brotherly affection.

Sometimes their fighting even proved valuable to their act. The best example of that occurred the day they were preparing to open at the Hollywood Paramount.

They were just winding up their *klabyash* game. Moe, the clear loser, still had a full hand of cards. But Shemp and Larry were down to a card apiece. Shemp put his down: an eight of diamonds. If Larry couldn't take it, it would be a tie. But he had an ace of spades and picked up the last trick.

"Guess I gotcha," he smiled.

"You did, eh?" roared Shemp. He stood and jammed two fingers into Larry's eyes.

Larry, from *Rockin' in the Rockies* (1945).

Moe actually fell off his chair in hysterics. Moe thought it was the funniest thing he had ever seen, but it took a while for Larry to see the humor in the situation. He was surprised he could see anything at all. Shemp felt pretty bad about it and apologized profusely. Larry's eyes were watery for days.

"We gotta put that in the show," Moe gasped when his laughter had subsided a bit.

"Are you crazy?" Larry yelled. "That god damn brother of yours nearly blinded me!"

"Don't worry, Fuzzy," said Moe. "We'll fake it. I'll practice on Shemp till I get it down."

Shemp wasn't too thrilled about that, but Moe was onto something and was not to be denied. Luckily for Shemp, Moe was a natural-born eye poker. No matter how fast he did it, his fingers always hit just beneath the eyebrows but safely above the eyes.

And thus was born the two-fingered Sign of the Stooge.

Larry never told this story without adding a warning, and I won't break with his tradition:

Kids! Don't try this trick yourselves! It should only be attempted by professional idiots.

TED HEALY VERSUS
HOWARD, FINE AND HOWARD ～～～～～1930

Ted Healy was vacationing in New York when a call from his agent shattered his tranquility: "Listen, Ted. The word from California is that your boys are doing your act out there on their own."

At first, Healy was numb with disbelief. The boys were just supposed to be soaking a little more of the California sun with their wives.

"I hear they're upset that you scotched some deal they had going with Fox," his agent went on.

Suddenly, it made sense: the boys had found out about Healy's chat with Sheehan and were trying to get even. The idea hit the Healy temper like a lit match in a gas tank.

"Sue 'em! Those boys were nothing when I found 'em! I'll see to it that they never work again!"

"Alright," said Healy's agent. "I'll have our lawyer on the Coast get right on it. But I want something from you in return."

"What's that?" snarled Healy.

"I want you to get back to work. Find some new stooges — whatever you have to do. But I want you onstage at the Palace by mid-September."

"The Palace?"

"They want you back, Ted. You were a smash. And no one argues with a smash."

Healy's agent was as good as his word. His Hollywood lawyer slapped a restraining order on Howard, Fine and Howard, and that temporarily closed the act.

Healy was at no loss for new stooges to bring to the Palace. His first step was to call his old pal, Dick Hakins. It was the only step he needed to take.

"You want three stooges, I'll give you three stooges," Dick told him. "We'll be on your doorstep tomorrow morning."

"Tomorrow *afternoon*," Healy corrected him. "If you know what's good for you."

The next day, Dick Hakins brought the comedy team of Jack Wolf and Paul "Mousie" Garner to meet Healy. And on September 15, the four of them found themselves headlining at the Palace.

The *New York Times* was moderately impressed:

> ...It is to be noted, but not with alarm, that a new aggregation of the ruffians quaintly called the Healy "Racketeers" has been enlisted. They are, at the moment, less menacing than Shemp Howard and his associated malefactors, but they are learning fast, and before you can drop a sandbag out of the flies, they will be thugs of the first order.

Ted Healy vs. Howard, Fine and Howard went to trial on September 30, 1930, in Los Angeles.

Howard, Fine and Howard came armed with an affidavit from Jake Shubert granting them the right to perform material from *A Night In Spain* and *A Night In Venice*. Their argument was this: since the Healy vaude act was virtually identical to the act they'd done for the Shuberts, the act's rightful owner wasn't Healy but the Shuberts.

Jake had been unusually magnanimous about signing the affidavit, but he had motives of his own. The courts were deciding more and more in favor of the authors in disputes between authors and producers. When someone recorded a song from a Shubert musical, it was the composer that got the royalties, and that drove Jake up the wall. Jake had already paid the composer to write the song. And now that his investment was paying off, the composer got paid again, and the Shuberts didn't get a dime. Jake figured that if Larry and the boys won the case, it would help support his contention that he owned Shubert-produced material.

Moe in foreground with (l. to r.): Shemp, unknown stage manager, Morris Feinberg, and Larry, backstage at the Earle Theatre in Philadelphia (1928). Note the sign warning performers about moonlighting: "To all artists: Your contract prohibits your appearance at any other place of entertainment during your engagement at the Earle Theatre."

Healy's lawyer decided to side-step this issue by claiming that the boys had stolen not only Healy's material but his comic style. It was a common practice in vaudeville for comedians to steal each others' jokes, but when they did, they were supposed to reinterpret them in terms of their own stage characters. If W.C. Fields stole a joke from Will Rogers, it would legitimately become a W.C. Fields joke by the new way he'd tell it. Healy's lawyer claimed that Moe Howard had gone far beyond such innocent trade-offs and had stolen Healy's entire stage character, nuance for nuance. Moe was merely doing a third-rate Healy imitation, and it had to be stopped.

Healy's lawyer presented his case well, but the court didn't go along with it. Moe might have delivered a lot of slaps, but he'd done that when working with Healy, too, and he never appeared as a comedian in his own right, apart from the other two. Moe wasn't so much the leader as the most violent in a trio of equals.

Case closed.

Larry closed his eyes with relief. But behind his closed eyelids shot a vision of Healy's cold fury. Larry shook his head and glanced at Shemp.

Shemp nodded his head: "I don't think we've seen the last of Ted Healy."

THE EARLE ～～～～～～～～～～～～～～～1930

Lovers of the vaudeville theater are forever telling us about the sculpted arches of the proscenium, the golden glow of the footlights, the wondrously elaborate sets that appeared out of nowhere to highlight a nine-minute act and vanished in a burst of applause. They're absolutely right: all that stuff was unforgettable. But I was a backstage fan, a fan of the secret corridors and the dressing rooms.

Now, I won't tell you that vaude dressing rooms were particularly glamorous or well-built. In fact, they were just the opposite: tiny, ill-lit, dirty. Naked light bulbs hung from the ceilings; rat droppings littered the corners. Even the ornate Shubert theaters had no hot tap water backstage. Here was the drab, hidden space, the shared adversity that brought the cast together into a family. And that's what I loved about it. Everyone was *mishpocheh* backstage; everyone was family. It was a family of performers, and, like any family, it was exclusive: maybe that's what made it so exciting. But it was generous enough to include brothers of performers as part of the gang.

Larry had been away on the West Coast for a lot longer than any of us had expected, and I had missed him and my backstage pass dearly. But the Howard, Fine and Howard act had obviously clicked: they'd picked up bookings at Paramount Theaters in San Francisco and Portland, signed with the William Morris agency and had worked their way back East. Finally, Larry and the boys arrived for a week's engagement at Philadelphia's Earle Theater, one of a rising breed of theaters that featured both live vaudeville and movies.

"So this is Philadelphia!" crowed Larry, spreading his arms in the middle of a dank dressing room. "It looks just like Hollywood!"

Larry and I were backstage, trading jokes with Moe Howard and biding our time till curtain.

"You're wrong, Fuzzy," said Moe, poking my brother in the eyes to keep in practice. "It looks like Detroit!"

Shemp was down the hall in his own dressing room. Larry and Moe, the extroverts of the group, always preferred to share a room. Visiting Larry and Moe backstage was as comfortable for me as visiting Larry alone. Moe would go out of his way to make me feel at home. But Shemp was more of a loner: I never quite got the "hang" of Shemp. Larry thought the world of both Howards, though, and that was good enough for me.

Larry and Moe were still debating which city most resembled their run-down dressing room when in walked a surprise guest, short as a stooge and elegant as a tycoon: Mr. Edward G. Robinson.

I was dumbfounded: Edward G. Robinson was one of the biggest stars of the "legit" stage. What was he doing in a vaude house?

"Listen, boys," he said. "If you can stick around after your show tonight, I'd like you to see my new picture as my guests."

Robinson was doing a stage play a few blocks away at the Locust, and he wanted his cast to see *Little Caesar*, which was due to open at the Earle the following week. He had made arrangements with the Earle for a special midnight preview. Everyone from the Locust and everyone from the Earle was invited — even the ushers, even Larry Fine's little brother. No one declined.

"And don't worry about dinner," Mr. Robinson added with

a wink. "The Horn and Hardart around the corner is gonna stay open for us." No one had to remind him that theater people tend to be famished after a show.

We all went back to our places. Robinson turned in another performance at the Locust. I claimed a seat at the Earle to watch Larry and company send another crowd into hysterics. By the time the show was over, Robinson had already returned with his cast. It was time for a party.

First, we marched over to the Horn and Hardart; there must have been at least 100 of us. The place was officially closed, but the manager let us in through a side door.

Horn and Hardart was the original "fast food" chain. They had restaurants and cafeterias all over New York and Philadelphia. Most of them were automats, where you got the food from nickel vending machines. The one near the Earle was an automat, but one of the better ones, with an excellent variety of hot food and sandwiches.

Edward G. Robinson went straight for the cashier's booth, got a mountain of nickels, and began passing them around. He was like a kid directing his own birthday party. I don't think he ate a thing: he was having too much fun running around from table to table making sure everyone had enough nickels.

It was a charming experience to be waited on by such a distinguished host, but the highlight of the evening was the screening itself, back at the Earle.

We were all taking our seats when who plunked down next to me but the star himself! I kept trying to call him "Mr. Robinson," but he would have none of it. "Call me Eddie," he insisted.

The house lights dimmed, and the picture began: a shadowy figure was walking down a dim-lit street.

Robinson turned to me and whispered in his gangster drawl, "I *get* this guy, see?"

Suddenly, the "rat-tat-tat" of a machine gun filled the air. The real Robinson was chuckling to himself with a diabolical, nasal laugh, while the movie Robinson was towering, gun in hand, over his victim.

It was great to see someone so clearly pleased with his work. When we gave him a standing ovation at the end of the picture, he was beaming: he actually seemed incandescent with joy.

As for myself, I can tell you that it was a very satisfied Moe Feinberg who drove his big brother home that night. It was five a.m., and I was bone-tired. But I had returned to the great fraternity of the backstage boys.

"Well, Larry," I said, "remember when we were kids, and we'd be fighting all the time, and I'd call you all those names? I take it all back. You're a damn good brother."

"Thanks, little brother," he said. Then he laughed and laughed.

THREE LOST SOULS ~~~~~~~~~~~~~ 1931

"Howard, Fine and Howard" was a pretty big mouthful for the name of a slapstick act. But Larry and the boys had more than that on their minds when they changed the name to "Three Lost Souls." As much as audiences enjoyed them, they were a problem-plagued group. And not the least of their troubles was a Mr. Ted Healy.

Healy had never forgiven the boys for going out on their own, and losing his lawsuit did nothing to abate his anger. He lobbied all his many contacts to boycott the boys, and, as a last resort, he phoned in bomb threats to theaters that booked the boys' act.

He didn't even bother to make the threat anonymous. "Hi! I'm Ted Healy," he'd say. "And if the 'Three Lost Souls' act goes on tonight, I'm going to bomb your theater."

Why he wasn't arrested, I'll never know. Larry, for one, didn't take the threats too seriously, but he had no choice but to take seriously the reactions of others. And almost everyone else was scared. Larry and Moe had to pay Shemp extra just to stay in the group. Many theaters refused to book them. Many more refused to book them again, once they were exposed to the full force of the Healy attack.

Larry would later refer to this period as his greatest struggle. In an interview with Twentieth Century Fox, he said: "We couldn't get work because Healy was always threatening to sue — or worse. I had my wife and child to take care of and was too proud to ask my folks for help. We missed a lot of meals. A man can stand that for himself, but not for his wife and children."

The "Three Lost Souls" act had aesthetic problems as well. They still weren't confident of their ability to work without a foil, someone to "stooge" off of. At the Paramount Theaters, they had used the emcees as their hapless leader/victims. But they couldn't always expect the emcee to take on so much of the burden of their act. Finally, they decided to hire a "straight man," a stereotypically tall, dark and handsome singer named Jack Walsh. The resulting act was funny enough, but they didn't get along very well. Moe considered him a transparent con artist. No tears were shed when they parted.

Jack Walsh, one of the early straightmen.
(from the collection of Mark Gilman.)

Healy, on the other hand, started out doing quite well without his renegade stooges. But then, he had a substantial reputation to fall back on.

He played the Palace so often and with such command that he became a kind of "super emcee." As the *New York Times* noted, "Mr. Healy could wring a cheer in advance for anyone."

But his new stooges were receiving mixed notices. Here's what the *New York Times* thought of Healy's Palace routine on November 24, 1930:

> The familiar Mr. Healy, whose new band of 'rack-
> eteers' now contains several young women, is
> amusing in, for him, a rather subdued fashion. Gone
> is much of the hilarious rough-house of his former,
> devil-may-care act, although efforts are made to
> recapture it by reviving one or two of the earlier
> Healy routines.

The *Times* was far friendlier with Healy's bunch when they appeared in *The Gang's All Here* at Broadway's Imperial Theater in January of 1931:

> Ted Healy, the tackling comic, is there with innum-
> erable grotesque stooges, who are funny enough to
> rejuvenate even a burlesque show.

But the *Times* turned peevish when the same crew appeared in *Crazy Quilt* a few months later at the 44th Street Theater. It noted, with regret, that Healy was used "tamely," and that his stooges followed him "nervously."

It wasn't that Healy's new stooges were less talented than our fave raves. They were all accomplished musicians and funny comedians. Perhaps they were *too* talented: how much talent is a stooge allowed to show? Unlike Larry and Fred Sanborn, Healy's new gang insisted on showcasing their musical talents. And that might have been too incongruous for fans of slapstick to swallow.

In any case, Healy was growing nostalgic for his old stooges by 1932. He was more than nostalgic, in fact: he was desperate. He was getting a divorce from Betty, his wife and vaude partner of ten years, and reports had it that he had crossed the line between serious drinking and alcoholism. He needed his old buddies around him again.

After consulting with his partners, Moe Howard decided to meet with Healy for a peace conference.

THE PASSING SHOW OF 1932 ～～～～～～～～～

Larry was elated when Moe and Healy struck a deal. Healy had promised to stop drinking, and the boys were to join him in a new Shubert musical: *The Passing Show of 1932*. At last, they could get on with their careers without the baggage of angry threats.

Shemp was more skeptical: "I told you I'd keep an open mind, Moe. And if that's what you wanna do, I guess I'll go along with it. But it ain't gonna last forever. You think he's still the kid we used to pal around with, but he isn't. He's a maniac!"

"He'll be all right once he cools out from all the booze," Moe assured him.

"Fine, fine," said Shemp. "But if he screws up once, just once, I'm gone. Get me?"

The deal, as far as Shemp was concerned, lasted for about two weeks. Healy was as good as his word when it came to drinking. But in the middle of rehearsals, when the show was preparing to hit the road for a trial run, Healy got another offer. The Balaban and Katz circuit wanted him as a headliner for a six-week tour at a substantially higher salary than he was to get in the *Passing Show.* So Healy presented Jake Shubert with an ultimatum: either give him top billing and a raise, or he was leaving the show. Jake not only threw him out of his office, he filed a lawsuit against him — which Jake eventually won. Courtrooms weren't exactly Healy's best venues.

Healy managed to convince Larry and Moe to go on the Balaban and Katz tour with him, but Shemp refused to discuss it.

"What do I care how they bill Ted Healy?" Shemp said to the boys. "What do I care how much they pay him? We get paid the same. I said I'd be in the *Passing Show,* and that's what I'm gonna do."

Larry and Moe were stuck. They didn't want to break up their trio, but they were worried about what might happen if all three of them were to stay with the *Passing Show.* Would Healy return to his drunken rage? It was an awful thought — worse than the idea of parting ways with Shemp. And what if they were able to convince Shemp to come along with them on the Balaban and Katz tour? It would only postpone the inevitable. Larry and Moe had forgiven Healy, but it was obvious that Shemp hadn't.

The team parted friends, but they parted.

The *Passing Show* opened in Detroit with Shemp as a kind of floating stooge. He didn't have his own act, but Jake used him throughout the show as comic relief.

Also on the bill was an energetic young veteran of the prestigious Keith Circuit named Joe Besser, who would later develop a funny bit as a loud and obnoxious sissy kid.

Detroit, though, wasn't impressed with the show, so it moved to Cincinnati for more tinkering. Nothing seemed to stem the tide of bad reviews.

After three weeks on the road, it closed for good, never reaching Broadway.

CURLY ~~~~~~~~~~~~~~~~~~~~~~ 1932

Healy had a hard time coming to grips with the fact that, even though he had won over Larry and Moe, Shemp was no longer one of his stooges. Shemp was the one he had been after in the first place!

But after a lukewarm opening in New York, Healy decided to seek out a new third Stooge. The material that Healy and the boys had developed over the years was designed for three stooges, not two. Wistful longing for Shemp wasn't going to change that.

Moe suggested they try another one of his brothers, a short, beefy guy named Jerry with long, wavy hair and a sweeping handlebar mustache. The Howard family had worked out well for Healy so far. He told Moe to send him around for an audition.

Jerry was the youngest of the Howards — six years younger than Moe and eight behind Shemp. Moe still occasionally called him "Babe," even though he was a mere year younger than Larry.

Jerry's drawback was stage experience. His only professional stint had been a comic relief bit for the Orville Knapp Band. The emcee would introduce him as a "guest conductor," and he'd strut out onstage in a breakaway tuxedo that would fall apart while he conducted the song.

Jerry was overjoyed by the chance to join the group and immediately dashed off to the theater for his audition. He did the Orville Knapp bit, but Healy was not impressed.

"Is that all he can do?" Healy asked Moe. "Let his pants fall down? Get me a real comedian — not this amateur. He doesn't even look right!"

Moe was still determined to get his brother into the act, so Moe and Larry got together with Jerry that night to teach him a few of their routines. Maybe if Healy could see them working well as a trio, he'd relent.

They also needed to address Healy's objection to Jerry's appearance. To be a stooge, you had to look like a stooge. Jerry's long locks and fancy mustache had served him well in the bandleader bit, but now he needed a look that was dramatically weird. If he looked outrageous enough, it might even cover for his lack of experience.

Moe suggested the ultimate stooge haircut, the knucklehead look, no hair at all.

"I can't cut off my hair!" Jerry stammered. "The girls love it! They wouldn't come near me if I was bald-headed!"

"Forget dames," said Moe. "You with us or not?"

"You're crazy!" Jerry was screaming. "How do we know Healy's gonna go for it? What if he doesn't give me another audition?"

"He'll give you another audition, all right," Moe smiled. "He probably won't know it's you. Mother won't even recognize you by the time we're through with you."

(l. to r.) Curly, Moe, Larry, & Ted Healy in rehearsal.
(from the collection of Steve Cox)

The next day, the boys arrived at the theater ahead of Healy and had Jerry wait in the wings. When Healy showed, they told him they'd found a "hot, new comedian, a real pro, the perfect replacement for Shemp." Then they went backstage and brought out one of the most ridiculous-looking fellows Healy had ever seen.

With his big, bald head and his pudgy features, the guy looked like a gigantic infant, the bastard son of King Kong and Fay Wray. And he had a tiny, Oliver Hardy-style mustache that was parted and waxed: a miniature handlebar.

His delivery was a little wooden and nervous. But he knew the act well, and it didn't throw him off when Moe and Larry started ad-libbing.

"Hey, Curly, come here," said Moe near the end of the act.

"What did you call him?" asked Larry.

"Curly, why?" replied Moe.

"That's all right. I thought you said, 'girlie'."

Healy bolted from his chair, yelling, "High class! High class! Let's keep that 'girlie' line!"

Healy bounded up onstage to shake the new guy's hand, which was already shaking with a clash of nervousness and relief. "What's your real name, Curly?"

Curly looked over at Larry and Moe, then back to Healy.

"It's Puss-head!" cracked Moe. "Puss-head Jones."

Curly's face clouded in fury. "I'm Jerry Howard," he snapped.

It wasn't easy to shock Ted Healy, but there he was: wide-eyed and open-mouthed. Larry and Moe were in hysterics.

"OK, you guys," said Healy. "You put one over on me, but he's hired."

KING OF STOOGES 〰〰〰〰〰〰〰〰〰 *1933*

Ted Healy and his new Howard, Fine and Howard gang got great notices on their tour. But signs of the death of vaudeville were everywhere: crowds were smaller, theaters were in disrepair, and everyone was talking about movies.

"Boys," Healy kept saying, "we gotta go back to Hollywood. We gotta start doing movies again."

When Healy and the boys returned to New York, they discovered that their renegade comrade, Shemp, had beaten them to the punch. Shemp had just signed a deal to make comedy shorts for Vitagraph, the only major studio still based in New York.

Healy was furious; Larry and Curly were petrified; Moe was firm. "Ted," Moe told him: "You take one drink, you make one threat against my brother, and we're through."

Healy's agent had the solution, though it didn't sound like much at first: an engagement at the New Yorker Cafe in the basement of the Hollywood Hotel.

An unknown fan, Larry, Moe, & Curly at a train station.
(from the collection of Steve Cox)

"You want me to play in a basement?" Healy shouted. "Where is this New Yorker Cafe, this Hollywood Hotel? In Des Moines? You want me to play in a basement in Des Moines?"

His agent assured him that the Hollywood Hotel was indeed in Hollywood, and that he would be untroubled by rats in its "basement." The New Yorker Cafe was a major gathering place for Hollywood's elite. It was the perfect place to develop contacts.

But there was still the perennial Healy problem of money. Our Mr. Show Biz had retained a room at New York's exclusive Lincoln Hotel for the entire time that he and the boys had been on tour. He had entrusted the keys to the place to one of his old drinking buddies, a steadfast member of the "beach" crowd that hung out in front of the Palace. So the room hadn't gone unused, but it had gone unpaid for.

Healy had just enough cash on hand to either pay for the room or provide everyone's fare to California. Of course, they were going to California. The problem was how to get Healy's belongings out of the Lincoln without paying for his room. Hotel-keepers tended to be suspicious of vaudevilleans with unpaid bills marching out of their hotels with large trains of suitcases and trunks.

But Ted Healy was resourceful: he brought the boys up to his room and had them each don two or three sets of his clothes, from underwear to overcoats. They didn't look impeccably tailored, to say the least. I'll never know why the desk clerk didn't spot them. Healy followed them out wearing three suits and a topcoat, and carrying a raincoat with every pocket bulging.

HOLLYWOOD ~~~~~~~~~~~ 1933

Larry had had many big stars in his audiences but never anything like the galaxy of luminaries that turned out for the boys' opening night at the New Yorker Cafe. The list was unbelievable: Clark Gable, Spencer Tracy, Jean Harlow, Buster Keaton, Carole Lombard....

"Nice, huh?" said Healy backstage. "But Clark Gable isn't going to hire us. We need Winnie Sheehan in that crowd. We need Louis B. Mayer. Those are the guys who are going to get us into the movie business."

"Picky, picky, picky," thought Larry, Moe and Curly.

Let me tell you that the boys were 100 percent satisfied with the Cafe crowd, both for its stature and its laughter. And they were pleased, for once, with their billing. No longer were they

105

anonymous "racketeers" or "Southern gentlemen." They were listed separately as "Howard, Fine and Howard."

As for breaking back into the movies, Larry figured the place to start was where they had left off. He decided to place a call to their old friend, Ben Stoloff — the guy who had directed *Soup to Nuts.*

"You know, Larry," said Stoloff. "It's good you called. Ted's right about playing for moguls: they're your ticket in this town. And I think I have just the connection for ya. A friend of mine — ever hear of Bryon Foy? Anyway, he's throwing a party for his new picture, and he just might be interested in a little live entertainment. Have Ted give Foy a call. Let me tell ya: there'll be moguls galore."

Bryon Foy's new film was *Are These Our Children,* an independent, low-budget feature, and Foy was desperately casting about for ways to get it distributed. He needed the umbrella of a major studio, so he had set up a screening for all the studio heads.

Foy was delighted with the idea of softening the old boys up with a little live slapstick, and so were Healy and the boys.

Some of you might find it odd that such a rowdy act would even be permitted at such an august gathering. But the studio heads of yesteryear weren't the Harvard-educated bankers you have today. Louis B. Mayer, boss of MGM, had entered the job market as a junk dealer. William Fox of Fox started as a clothes sponger. Columbia's Harry Cohn had been a song plugger like Larry. They had all become tough, savvy businessmen, but culturally, they were just plain folks. No chamber music for these guys: bring on the clowns!

The act was a smash: everyone expressed interest. Larry told me they talked the offers over that night. It was the first time they spoke to Harry Cohn. But if I know Healy, the talk couldn't have lasted long. MGM was the Grand Hotel of the studios: the one with the stars, the Academy Awards and the lavish musicals.

The next day, they met with Louis B. Mayer and signed with MGM.

According to Larry, their career at MGM got off to a shaky start with a short "so bad they burned it up without ever releasing it." In any case, *Nertzery Rhymes,* their first release, was a smash. It was shot in an experimental two-tone Technicolor — lots of reds and greens — that seemed custom-made to highlight Larry's reddish-brown hair and blue eyes. Larry and the boys were terrific as over-sized kids in a giant crib harassing their father, Ted Healy.

Moe, Curly, Bonnie Bonnell, Ted Healy, and Larry in *Nertzery Rhymes* (1933).
(from the collection of Greg & Jeff Lenburg)

All the shorts that the boys made with Healy were multi-faceted affairs alternating between a running slapstick situation and impressive kaleidoscopic dance numbers. They even managed to throw in a little romance. Healy had managed to include his new girlfriend, Bonnie Bonnell, in the deal, and now she was his screen sweetheart as well.

Larry's musical background came in handy for these shorts. Over the years, Larry had taught himself to play the piano and had even come to prefer it to the violin. When the chance came to capture his achievement on celluloid, he jumped on it. Healy and the boys had minor roles in *Dancing*

Lady, a lavish feature starring Clark Gable, Joan Crawford and Fred Astaire. Healy and the boys were to be various backstage characters, and Larry pleaded for the role of piano player. Joan Crawford, a veteran of the Shubert chorus line, interceded for him. Larry got the part, and Miss Crawford got a fan for life.

Healy and his slovenly comrades landed parts in five other features, and while the parts were all small, they played them to perfection. Reviewing *Meet The Baron,* a comedy starring Jimmy Durante and Jack Pearl, the "Baron Munchausen" of radio fame, *Variety* claimed: "Healy, the Howards, and Larry Fine, left to their own methods, pretty nearly steal the picture."

Other studios began acknowledging the team's popularity. Paramount used them in one of their *Hollywood on Parade* shorts, and a film of their off-stage antics turned up on Columbia's *Screen Snapshots* series.

Bryon Foy, their old benefactor, managed to borrow them from MGM long enough for a feature, *Myrt and Marge,* starring radio's popular mother-and-daughter team, Myrtle Vail and Donna Damerel. It was released by Universal to vanish in a swarm of bad reviews. Only Healy and his stooges

Larry, Moe, Curly, and Ted Healy in *Myrt and Marge* (1934).
(from the collection of Jeff and Greg Lenburg)

escaped the critical scolding "by sticking to their own vaudeville technique," as *Variety* put it.

The Depression year of 1933 had been a busy one for Larry
and the boys. It had been even busier for Healy. For every
feature film he made with his stooges, he made another without them. In *Lazy River,* he even became a stooge himself,
playing a mad lackey to Robert Young. That was fine with
Larry: it gave him a chance to visit the racetrack. But Moe
was suspicious: were they supposed to be a team or what?

The thing that bothered all three of Healy's stooges was
money. Here they were working in Hollywood's most lavish
studio, and they were still only getting $100 a week. The prob-
lem was that they weren't working for the studio. They were
working for Healy.

Healy and the boys kicked off 1934 by appearing in a
Jimmy Durante/Laurel and Hardy vehicle called *Hollywood
Party.*

Logo for Jimmy Durante, the famous "Shnozzle".

Durante was something of a disappointment at MGM. In
vaudeville, he had been the great Schnozzola, the gravelly-
voiced tormentor of the English language and composer of
such ragtime classics as "Toscanini, Stokowski and Me"
and "Inka Dinka Doo." But his movies were invariably pan-
ned by the critics and ignored at the box office. Rumors

(l. to r.) Madge Evans, Larry, Moe, Curly, and Nate Pendleton from *Fugitive Lovers* (1934).

floated around the set that Durante's days at MGM were numbered if *Hollywood Party* didn't take off.

Healy contemplated the rumors with glee: "They must have some more stories lying around for Durante," he said. "Who's gonna do 'em, if he's gone?"

It didn't take a wizard to figure what that meant. Durante didn't work with stooges.

When Healy's contract came up for renewal on March 6, the boys added Healy's new ambitions up with their own financial dissatisfaction and decided on a bold move.

"Listen, Ted," Moe said. "Let's just break up. No hard feelings, no sneaking around. Just a good, clean split."

Healy agreed, and on the Ides of March, the King of Stooges found himself stoogeless, practicing his Durante imitation in an empty room.

COLUMBIA YEARS

Harry Cohn was the only studio head in Hollywood to hold both the chief of production job and the presidency of his company.

Cohn had broken into the movie business at the age of 27 by devising a clever boost to the art of song-plugging. Instead of just putting the words on slides as Larry's old boss Emmett Welsh and others had done, Cohn filmed little stories to fit the lyrics of the songs. Irving Berlin's publishing company, for whom Cohn had once worked as a plugger, became one of his enthusiastic clients. Nowadays, we might think of Cohn's little half-reelers as the precursors of the "rock video."

After a brief stint at Carl Laemmle's Universal Studio, Cohn formed an independent production company called C.B.C. with his brother Jack and a family friend, Joe Brandt. Cohn insisted that "C.B.C." stood for "Cohn, Brandt and Cohn," but Hollywood preferred to think of them as "Corned Beef and Cabbage." Eventually they decided to change the name to Columbia.

The company's first project was *Screen Snapshots*: a series of newsreel-style shorts showing the off-duty antics of celebrities. The frugal partners enjoyed the idea of using big-name stars for free. The series ran for nearly twenty years.

Of course, they also made comedy shorts. One popular series starred Billy West as a letter-perfect Chaplin imitation. Another series was based on the *Hall Room Boys* comic strip. They did well enough that within two years, the company was making features.

Most independent studios started out in the forlorn block of Beechwood Drive known as Poverty Row and left as soon as they could. Columbia bought it and made it a cornerstone of its empire along with "Gower Gulch" a block away and the strip of Sunset Boulevard that connected them. Thus Columbia came to be called the "Poverty Row studio."

By 1934, Harry Cohn had beaten an attempt by Jack Cohn and Joe Brandt to depose him. Joe Brandt was gone; Jack was vice-president and treasurer, far away in New York. And Harry was the undisputed boss of a major studio.

Larry and the boys had run into Mr. Cohn at Bryon Foy's party and a few months later at a sneak preview for *It Hap-*

Larry, the movie star, in an early Columbia publicity photo
(from the collection of Steve Cox.) © 1984 Columbia Pictures Industries, Inc.

pened One Night, Columbia's first strong bid for an Academy Award. Not only was it directed by *wunderkind* Frank Capra, who had given Coumbia a flawless string of romantic comedies, it starred two of the biggest draws in Hollywood: Clark Gable and Claudette Colbert. Big names were a rarity at Columbia, and Cohn had had to beg Louis B. Mayer for the use of Gable.

It was going to take an Oscar to heal Cohn's wounded pride. But what if the film were to bomb, bomb so badly as to

Moe, Larry, unknown man, and Curly.
(from the collection of Steve Cox)

render its Oscar ambitions a joke? Healy and the boys had been in a movie with a distressingly similar storyline at MGM called *Fugitive Lovers*. And it had been hooted out of the theaters.

The screening of Cohn's gamble had been a public one, and Cohn hadn't counted on seeing any familiar faces besides his own entourage as they made their way out of the theater. But when he chanced upon Larry and the Howards in the lobby, the powerful vaude fan stopped a moment.

"Well, boys," he said. "What did you think of the picture?"

"It was great," said Larry.

Cohn shoved the boys aside. "It stinks," he snorted and Harry Cohn was gone.

Remember now, the boys were in the market for a new studio. After this encounter, Columbia was on the bottom of the list. But it was a short list, and after a few "no"s and fewer "maybe"s, our fearful threesome found themselves once again face-to-face with Harry Cohn. But by now many people had told Cohn that *It Happened One Night* was destined for great things and he remembered Larry's original, favorable review.

"It's my good luck boys!" Cohn cheered to his startled supplicants. "You were right about *It Happened One Night*. Now what can I do for you?"

Larry, Curly, and Moe, without their signature haircuts, from *The Captain Hates the Sea* (1934). (from the collection of Mark Gilman.)

Larry would always say that they settled on a handshake: "You don't need a contract with me, boys!" he'd bellow in imitation of the bellicose Mr. Cohn. "As long as I'm president, you've got a job at Columbia!"

But that was just Larry's line to get out of discussing his contract at dinner parties. He hated talking business.

Moe Howard led the boys down to the legal department and settled on a 60-day deal for a short and a role in a feature. If it worked out to everyone's satisfaction, they'd get yearly contracts.

Their eventual contract had an interesting payment scheme. They were paid regular paychecks like salaried staff — as if they were reporting for 40-hour work weeks 48 weeks a year to make an annual output of eight shorts. Of course, if the Stooges had ever lingered longer than four days on a short, they would have been given the bum's rush. But to the bookkeeping department, it took six weeks to make a short. The extra time was free — time to raise their families, to gamble, to tour.

Still, there was some truth to Larry's handshake story. The boys did shake hands with Cohn, and the loyalty of Harry Cohn, the old song-plugger, held them in better stead over the years than many a contract.

THE THREE STOOGES~~~~~~~~~~~~~~~~1934

Larry and the boys worked in Lewis Milestone's *The Captain Hates The Sea,* filmed on location, like today's *Love Boat,* on the high seas. They were colorful extras on a wild Hollywood cruise that turned out to be more of a party than a production.

Cohn cabled the crew: "Hurry up. The cost is staggering."
The director wired back: "So is the cast."

Jules White, the dapper producer of the shorts department, associated the boys with musicals because of their work with MGM. So, once back in the studio, Larry and the Howards found themselves in a curious "singing comedy" called *Woman Haters.*

Curly and Moe weren't too crazy about it, but Larry kind of liked it. He had the leading role, for one thing. And his leading lady, Marjorie White, was a knockout.

When they got together after screening the final rushes, Moe decided it was time for a serious discussion.

First off, *Woman Haters* was a musical with all its dialogue in rhymed verse. It was an interesting novelty, but perhaps it was too novel. To gather fans, they needed a repeatable style. If people were going to look forward to the next Howard, Fine and Howard flick, they needed to know what to expect. The boys needed a *schtick,* a unique bag of tricks, and they knew it wasn't going to be singing in rhymed couplets.

117

(top to bottom) Larry, Moe, and Curly
in publicity still for *Swing Parade of 1946.*
(from the collection of Mark Gilman)

Their second concern was even more basic: were they going to be a team or just three guys who happen to be in the same movies all the time? In the Healy shorts, they were always three of a kind: three waiters, three brothers, three horn-players. Each of them had their unique eccentricities, but they were clearly cut from the same cloth. It was as if something had gone hilariously wrong with a cloning experiment.

But in *Woman Haters,* they had totally separate roles. They were the Three Ted Healys. And that wasn't a team.

Moe talked Columbia into letting them do one more short before negotiating their annual contract. It was to be a short they'd write themselves to demonstrate the type of comedy they wanted to do.

The short was *Punch Drunks.* In it, Moe and Larry discover that "Pop Goes The Weasel" sends Curly into an uncontrollably violent rage. Moe turns boxing promoter and puts Curly in the ring while Larry lurks nearby to play the magic melody on his violin. Together, they knock the boxing world on its ear.

One more matter remained: what was this Howard, Fine and Howard business? It sounded like a music publishing house, or even worse, a law firm. They needed a name.

Moe finally piped up: "Hell, we're stooges, ain't we? So why not call us "The Three Stooges"?

And so they did. And so they were.

Curly, Moe, and Larry in an early Three Stooges' give-away card.

MEN IN BLACK ～～～～～～～～～ *1934-1935*

One of the most talked about entertainments of 1934 was a gritty, sentimental Broadway play called *Men In White*. A hospital drama by Sidney Kingsley, it set the formula for nearly all future medical shows from *Young Doctor Kildare* to *Marcus Welby, M.D.*: the old/young doctor relationship, the passion for medical terms, the soap-opera plot. Within nine months after its Broadway opening, it won a hotly-contested Pulitzer Prize and spawned a high-budget screen adaptation starring Clark Gable and Myrna Loy.

Many considered the prize outrageous: "No future Pulitzer Prize will be good for anything but a hearty laugh," fumed A.E. Thomas in the *New York Herald Tribune*.

Enter the Three Stooges.

Dr. Howard, Dr. Fine and Dr. Howard gave the play some hearty whiffs of laughing gas, twisted its innards and came up with *Men In Black*.

The spoof was so successful, it was nominated for an Academy Award as "Best Comedy Short." Ironically, the cloyingly serious adaptation with Clark Gable and company was completely ignored by the Academy.

James Cagney, in charge of entertainment for the presentation ceremony, asked the boys to perform, and they accepted in a flash.

On the night of the Awards, February 27, 1935, the Stooges did a fast-moving pastiche of their old vaude bits before an overflow crowd of nearly a thousand guests at the Biltmore Bowl of Hollywood's Biltmore Hotel.

As they were leaving the stage that night, a jovial Henry Fonda shook their hands and said, "I've been a fan of yours ever since I saw you in New York. I hope you win your Oscar tonight."

But alas, our heroes were defeated at the hands of *La Cucaracha,* an RKO musical in the mold of the Healy shorts.

The next Award given that night was "Best Cartoon." Walt Disney won it for *The Tortoise And The Hare,* and Harry Cohn was furious. Four years earlier, Disney had been making cartoons for Columbia, but Disney and the volcanic Mr. Cohn had gotten into a bitter dispute, and Disney had quit. To Cohn's way of thinking, Disney was supposed to be crawling back on his hands and knees, not winning Oscars for his own production company.

Cohn ran into Larry and grabbed him by the lapels: "So how come Disney wins an Oscar, and you don't? Huh?"

Larry was flabbergasted: "But we weren't even in competition! It was a totally different award!"

Cohn waved him off and plunged back into the crowd in search of new victims. But Larry was so shocked by the incongruity of Cohn's demand that for the rest of his life, he would tell people that the Stooges had been beaten by Disney.

Harry Cohn, on the other hand, was to forget he'd even heard of Disney by the end of the night. *It Happened One*

Night didn't just win an Oscar, it *swept* them! It won "Best Actress," "Best Actor," "Best Director," and finally, Cohn's personal award, "Best Picture."

Larry had something to crow about as well: Ted Healy had bet him that MGM's Norma Shearer would take "Best Actress." Larry had gone for Claudette Colbert in *It Happened One Night* and won. The Stooges were company men at last. And the Columbia Picture Company was on the upswing.

THE EARLE (Reprise) ~~~~~~~~~~~~~~~~1935

The Stooges rarely made personal appearances during the two years that they spent establishing themselves in Hollywood. But now the offers were pouring in: quality offers to headline in big-time venues like the Orpheum in Los Angeles.

Just between you and me, Larry and the boys were a little scared: they had never been headliners without Healy. They decided a little "try-out" tour of familiar theaters might be just the thing to get the rust out and break in some new material.

They arranged a booking at the Earle Theatre in Philadelphia.

The boys weren't scheduled to open till Monday night, but they arrived the Friday before, filled with ideas and anxious to get to work.

They didn't want the Earle's backstage crowd looking over their shoulders while they were working out their new bits, so they came to our house to rehearse. The three of them spent the weekend planning the act in my bedroom.

I left them alone every once in a while, but I had to help a *little,* didn't I?

One of the old bits they used to do in their "Three Lost Souls" act was a fast-paced game of charades with the emcee. Larry would just stand still, and the exasperated emcee would ask him what he was doing.

"Going upstairs," Larry would say.

"Going upstairs?"

"Yeah, I'm in an elevator!"

It was a funny bit, but I thought it would be funnier if they scrapped the charades part and announced it as a new dance craze: the Elevator.

"Right!" laughed Larry. "It's got no steps!"

The Stooges were nominally the "next-to-closing" act, but the emcee had a little blackout bit — a few songs — between the Stooges and the closing act. Both the Stooges and the dance team that did "closing" used full stage, so they needed a little filler while they did the set-ups backstage.

The closing act was very imposing. It began with a ballet by two young guys to soft Egyptian music. Then two black strongmen arrived, dressed in loin cloths and Egyptian headdresses and carrying a mummy case. They set the case down on center stage and froze in "cigar-store Indian" poses. The ballet dancers opened the case, and a breathtakingly beautiful woman emerged. The three of them broke into a wild dance based on the "Pandora's Box" theme while the strongmen gazed vacantly at the audience.

The show was pretty tightly timed, but the Stooges were ad-libbing a lot and experimenting with different routines, so they never finished at the same time each night. The emcee had to shorten his own act whenever the Stooges ran over. But he never abbreviated it without screaming at the Stooges and complaining to the manager.

The Stooges and the guys from the dance act got together and devised a plan to get even with him. The dance act boys had no particular beef with the emcee, but they saw the chance to play a practical joke on their charming partner, and they just couldn't resist.

On Saturday night, the last night of the boys' run at the Earle, the Stooges did an extra-long set to get the emcee in the mood for the mayhem to follow. While the emcee was singing the one song he had time to do, the boys did a quick change. The woman in the dance act was already in her mummy-case: she said it helped her get in the right frame of mind to perform.

It wasn't the strongmen that carried the mummy case on-stage. It was the Three Stooges, naked but for towels round their waists, Egyptian headdresses and their shoes and socks. The woman inside must have wondered what all the laughter was about.

She found out soon enough: the case opened to reveal three clowns in place of her partners. For her, the rest of the show was a laughing jag as she let herself be thrown from Stooge to Stooge in a dance they never taught in ballet school. The audience was howling and whistling.

The emcee came out and tried to get the boys off the stage.

"Look, fellas," cried Curly, "it's another stooge for our act!"

Larry and the boys grabbed him and started undressing him right there on stage. By the time the startled stage manager thought to pull the curtain, the screaming emcee was down to his birthday suit, and the crowd was roaring its approval.

Moe, Larry, and Curly surrounded by four unknown gentlemen.
(from the collection of Steve Cox)

The next time the Stooges appeared at the Earle, they brought their own emcee: Eddie Laughton, Larry's old friend from the "Haney Sisters and Fine" days. Larry loved to share his success with those of us who "knew him when," and Eddie proved to be an excellent straight man for the Stooges.

Back in Hollywood, Larry helped Eddie get started in a pleasant career playing characters with names like "Footsy" and "Measles" in grade-B gangster epics for Columbia.

ATLANTIC CITY ～～～～～～～～～～～～～ *1936*

It looked as if Larry was going to be seeing a lot of Hollywood for awhile, but he and Mabel still thought of themselves as residents of Atlantic City.

They had considered buying a house in Los Angeles when Healy and the boys first landed the MGM deal, but a good-sized earthquake had gotten in the way. Mabel never really got over the terror she'd felt. The only way she could bear to be in California at all was to think of herself as rooted in Atlantic City.

"It's the people who live here who need to worry about earthquakes," she told herself. "Tourists are safe."

It didn't make much sense, but it worked. Larry and Mabel made their home in Atlantic City's posh President Hotel overlooking the boardwalk. And when visiting California, they'd check into the Knickerbocker.

In March of 1936, the Fines were vacationing in Hollywood, making movies and stuff, when another citizen of Atlantic City was born in L.A.'s Wilshire Hospital: Johnny Fine.

Little Phyllis, all of seven years old, was delighted: she had asked for a poodle, but a baby brother was even better. It confirmed her image of her parents as very shrewd operators indeed. Living in hotels was like a constant holiday what with maid service and no responsibilities. She was surprised that it hadn't occurred to more people to live that way.

Atlantic City's Steel Pier was a blockbuster building jutting boldly over the ocean — a man-made peninsula with a man-made sky under which every conceivable kind of family entertainment was performed constantly and simultaneously. A single admission granted you access to two theaters, a ballroom, carnival rides, circus acts and more.

The Steel Pier marquee headlining The Three Stooges.

The Stooges were booked into the Steel Pier so regularly that they were more of a tradition than an act. Every year, they played the two biggest weekends: Memorial Day and Labor Day. Summer wasn't summer till the Stooges played the pier, and it wasn't over till they returned.

Even the bits they did became kind of traditional. Once they settled on their act, they did little to change it. It seemed that the audiences wanted them to do all the old jokes: they expected the obvious and were pleased when they got it.

It was at the Steel Pier that I first realized just how successful my big brother had become.

The Stooges were appearing with the stars of my favorite radio show, Burns and Allen. I had been a fan of theirs ever since they first wafted over the airwaves on 1932's *Eddie Cantor Show*. By 1936, all America was their fan.

125

George Burns & Gracie Allen from "The Philadelphia Record,"
January 3, 1937
(Courtesy of the Free Library of Philadelphia: Arthur Soll, Research Photographer)

When my new bride, Dinah, and I saw the marquee at the Steel Pier, you could have knocked us over with a dream. Who do you think was the headliner? Not Burns and Allen. It was the Three Stooges that dominated the bill, with Burns and Allen in smaller type below.

Larry was again pressed into service as my human backstage pass. With luck, I thought, I might even meet my radio idols, the Stooges' opening act.

Luck, nothing. It would have been hard to avoid George Burns: he was everywhere at once, *kibbitzing* with everyone on the bill. He was the most happy-go-lucky guy I'd ever met, and — considering my brother — that was saying a lot. As soon as he met me, he treated me as if we'd been kids together playing tricks on the teacher.

I wrote him about this book. "Hang in there, kid," he says. See, I'm a kid to him. I'm only 80 years old.

But you never saw Gracie unless George escorted you to their dressing room. She was the funniest comedienne in the world, bar none. But in person, she exuded vulnerability. She

126

was so shy and reserved that, right away, you wanted to protect her from the ravages of the outside world.

Watching her onstage that night, I realized that her vulnerability was a vital, if unconscious, aspect of her act. Some comics — the Three Stooges would be the best example — invoked an almost derisive laughter: "Ha! Ha! Look at the knuckleheads!" But Gracie produced a laughter filled with a yearning to shelter her that could tear you apart.

Meeting big stars backstage was always a highlight of visiting Larry in Atlantic City. But no visit with Larry was complete without a trip to the gambling dens, the illicit back rooms.

"Who's your friend?" someone asked Larry.

"Ever hear of rabbit's feet?" Larry said. "He's got two human ones. Actually, he's my little brother."

Curly, Larry, and Moe with hand puppets, 1935.

Everyone fell down laughing, but at least I was accepted.

Larry was shooting craps and doing pretty well when a guy named Harry stepped from the shadows. Larry turned from the craps game and handed him a slip of paper and a bundle of cash.

"Here's the bets," he said. "They're solid."

It was a monstrous bet: there were three tracks with eight races in a track, and Larry had picked the winner in every race. But Harry got it all confused: he bet the wrong horses.

Whether he was losing a bundle at the track, *kibbitzing* backstage with George Burns or handling his personal affairs, Larry was the same jovial imp. His gambling motto was this: "Easy come, easy go."

The first question people usually ask about the Stooges is this: "Did they ever hurt themselves while they were bashing each other around?"

As long as they stuck to their old vaude staples of poking, slapping and kicking each other, they were fine. They never got hurt onstage. But in the movies, other people — unschooled in slapstick — got to join in the mayhem. Slaps by women were the worst: they tended to keep their fingers too stiff and hit too high up on the side of the face.

(l. to r.) Vernon Dent, Curly, Larry, Moe, and Paul Kruger from *Idiots Deluxe* (1945).

Then there were the stunts. In vaudeville, you'd have a stunt or two that you knew perfectly and could repeat for years. But the movies required new and dangerous-looking bits of business every day. Even though the Stooges were careful to work with first-rate special effects men, accidents had to happen sooner or later.

In one picture, Moe was supposed to hit Larry with a soft rubber hammer — a safe enough trick for such seasoned vets of combat comedy. But the handle was wooden, and it was the handle that connected with Larry's tubular nose, breaking it.

"You look great, Larry," enthused Moe. "Mousier than ever!"

The boys were carpenters in 1935's *Pardon My Scotch*. Moe was standing on a table measuring shelves while Larry and Curly used the table as a sawhorse. Of course, they were not only sawing through their piece of wood but the table as well, which had been wired to break away. The idea was this: the propman would pull the wire, causing the table to break neatly in two and allowing Moe to tumble safely through the middle.

But when the wire was pulled, the table didn't break: it flipped over, throwing Moe in the air to land on one of its upturned legs. He broke three ribs.

The film that really brought out the ambulances, though, was *Three Little Pigskins*. The climactic scene called for our diminutive heroes to be tackled by an entire football team — real football players from Loyola University. Larry was having no part of it and insisted on using doubles.

"Come on, Larry," said producer Jules White. "You boys know how to take a fall. Doubles aren't in the budget."

"This ain't no fall," Larry protested. "It's an avalanche! We'll be buried alive!"

Larry and the boys prevailed, and when the scene was over, two of the new Stooge doubles and four bystanders had broken arms and legs.

From that day on, Jules White thought to include a provision for doubles when budgeting Stooge flicks.

Lucille Ball made one of her first screen appearances in the ill-fated but hilarious *Three Little Pigskins*. "The only thing I learned from the Three Stooges," she'd say, recalling the chaos, "was how to duck!"

BUNGLED BIRTHDAYS ~~~~~~~~~ *1939*

Early in 1939, I got a call from Larry asking if I could go to City Hall and get him a birth certificate.

"What's up?" I asked. "Some sucker bet you guys don't exist?"

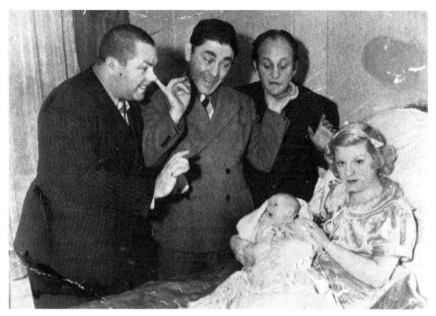

Curly, Moe, and Larry with Mabel, Larry's wife, and newborn Phyllis Fine.

"Yeah," Larry laughed. "Wanna buy in on it? No, serious-ly, Moe: I need to get a passport. We're gonna play Europe — the Palladium, gay Paree, the works!"

OK, I was impressed. The next day, I strolled down to the Department of Records to check in on my pal Billy Tuckman, who just happened to be a Vital Statistics Clerk.

Billy and I did a lot of amateur theater with the YMHA. They had a club that did all-male shows like the old Mask and Wig group. Since Billy was a short guy with a high-pitched voice, he always wound up playing one of the chorus girls. He was a riot, and he had a great set of gams.

I told him that Larry and I had always celebrated our birth-days on the same day, September 5, and that Larry was two years older. Billy took out the book for September, 1902, but couldn't find any entry for any "Louis Feinberg," Larry's original name.

"You sure about the date?" he asked.

"Sure, I'm sure! I'm his brother, ain't I?"

"Well, it's not here," he sighed. "I'm gonna check August and October. You better pray you're wrong, and it's in one of those. The last guy we couldn't find, we made him get sworn statements from everyone he ever knew. His hair turned white overnight."

Billy had a penchant for exaggeration, but I got his drift. I took his advice and prayed I was wrong. Boy, how I prayed!

He found it under October 5th: so that was Larry's real birthday! I pumped Billy's hand in feverish gratitude.

The Lord, I thanked later.

Larry never let this quirk of municipal bookkeeping change his birthday celebration, however. If September the 5th was good enough for the first 37 years of his life, it was good enough for the rest, too.

Curly, Larry, and Moe.
(from the collection of Steve Cox.)

World War II gun emplacements on the Queen Mary.
(from the collection of Queen Mary Archives, Wrather Port Properties.

THE PALLADIUM ～～～～～～～～～～～～～～ *1939*

Larry and the boys were set to open at the London Palladium on June 5, but as the date approached, plans to extend the tour onto the European mainland evaporated. Hitler's Germany was clearly in an expansive mood, and Europe had a bad case of the jitters. Germany had reoccupied the Rhineland and annexed parts of Czechoslovakia and Austria in March. Now, in May, they had signed a "Pact of Steel" with Italy, which had just annexed Albania. Everyone wondered just how far Hitler and Mussolini were planning to go, how long the world could watch the map of Europe being eaten up without going to war. The Stooges decided to stick to the British Isles, England and Ireland, a step away from the powderkeg.

Mother had the same qualms about her little Larry performing in war zones that she had shown in the First World War.

"There ain't gonna be no war, Ma," Larry tried to assure her.

What really set her fears to rest — or rather, thrilled her to distraction — was the sight of the ship that was to spirit Larry and the gang away. It was the Queen Mary, crown of the Cunard Line, a floating palace.

Celebrities were a commonplace to this majestic ship. Besides the Stooges, the names of George Raft, Douglas Fairbanks, and a host of tycoons and royalty glittered on the passenger list. But the biggest star was the ship herself. People lined the docks to see her.

Larry and Mabel took Mother, Lyla and me to their suite aboard the ship, and I found myself pacing the length of it, shouting, "This is big! Big! Big!" The suite alone was as big as a yacht.

"All ashore that's going ashore," came the call.

"You better watch me close," I told Larry. "Or you'll have a stowaway on your hands."

He laughed: he thought I was kidding. Mother and Lyla led me to the dock, just in case.

Too soon, we found ourselves waving at a scene straight out of the movies: the Three Stooges waving and clowning with Mabel Fine and Helen Howard at the railing. Poor Curly had gotten into a spat with his wife Elaine and was alone on this trip. But it was Curly the Clown that "accidently" hit Moe in the face as he exuberantly bid his adieu.

London audiences went nuts over the Stooges, raising the rafters with laughter, but the critics were more, ah, critical. Lionel Hale, for example, expressed "wonder" that "the audience seemed most to enjoy the Americans and the savage assault on their ears."

Adjusting his monocle, Mr. Hale cast a baleful eye upon the three specimens of *Vaudeville Americanus* in the light of England's Music Hall tradition:

> Music Hall and Vaudeville — what a difference! Yet no matter how we sigh for the warm, plush, good-natured vulgarity of the old halls, what we have now is a bright, brassy, hard, Americanized, wry, acid business.

And what the theatre managers say to us is, in effect, what Mr. Pickwick is accused of saying to Mrs. Bardwell: 'You're a good creature; compose yourself to this situation, for to this situation you must come.'

....There is a sort of shuddering fascination about [the Stooges]. They make themselves creatures of the dustbin, endowed with a restless, brazen, cruel wit. They are funny; and there is no fun in them.

Another clipping from the boys' Palladium adventure, forwarded by London's Mander and Mitchenson Theatre Collection, is friendlier but just as distant:

Though their humor is sometimes definable, it is more often more mystifying than anything the Marx Brothers have to offer; and the nonsense that Lear and Carroll fathered seems with them to have cast off its last connexion with sense. Nonsense has seldom had so appreciative a public as it has today... but the true enjoyment of the 'Stooges' seems to require immoderate folly in the audience.

"Immoderate folly" seemed to pose no problem for London audiences, and the boys were held over for a spectacular second week.

Eveywhere they went — Blackpool, Dublin, Glasgow — the Stooges drew huge, gleeful crowds, and offers for still more engagements were pouring in. But the boys had already signed to appear in George White's *Scandals of 1939* back in the States.

Sadly, it was time for *Vaudeville Americanus* to return to its native habitat.

It seems that every time we Feinbergs try to get from the Old World to the New, the ships are packed. Mother and Dad had been forced to contend with overloaded immigrant steamers. Now, with Hitler threatening to invade Poland and bomb shelters being erected in London, even the Queen Mary was crowded with people anxious to put an ocean between themselves and the worsening crisis. All the staterooms were reserved, but the Stooges and their wives decided to book passage anyway, even if it meant sleeping in the dining room.

Poster for the London Palladium.
(from the collection of Stoll Moss Theaters, Ltd.)

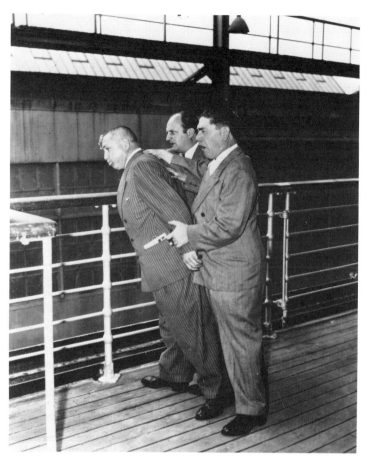

Curly, Larry, and Moe on deck, from *The Captain Hates the Sea* (1934).

A glance at the changes that the Queen Mary had undergone in the past month confirmed everyone's view of the urgency of their departure: a cannon had been mounted, and a gun crew was aboard in case of attack.

Fortunately, Lord Beaverbrook and his entourage had been forced to cancel their reservations at the last moment, and the Stooge families were able to take over his abandoned suites. And aside from the titters of excitement that came from the occasional U-boat sightings, it was a trouble-free crossing.

But the Stooges had made a timely escape. In little more than a month, Hitler made good on this threat to invade Poland, and Allied shipping was being destroyed all over the Atlantic.

For a dazzling quarter of a century, Broadway had been dominated by a string of lavish revues: the Ziegfeld *Follies,* which ran from 1907 to 1929, the Shuberts' *Passing Shows* of 1913 to 1924, Earl Carroll's *Vanities,* which had marked Ted Healy's Broadway debut in 1925, and George White's *Scandals.* Common to all were high production values, fast-paced, naughty gags, and girls, girls, girls.

Now the era was all but over. The mighty Ziegfeld had died bankrupt in 1932, and the Shuberts' *Passing Show* of the same year hadn't made it to its own New York opening. George White had fled the stage to begin a new career in the movies.

It hardly seemed right for such an extravagant form of entertainment to putter out so pathetically. It was out of synch with its own format: you had to go out with a bang; leave 'em laughin'; bring the whole cast onstage for a grand finale. And so it was that the ghosts of old Broadway finally lured George White back East to launch one more *Scandals* show, a last hurrah for the magic that had ignited a generation.

George White was to be assisted in this amazing endeavor by an "all-star" cast of 77, including our own Three Stooges. As soon as the boys hit Manhattan harbor, they went straight for Atlantic City to begin rehearsals.

It had been nearly a decade since a Broadway-bound production had used Atlantic City as a "try-out town," and the grateful city was prepared to cheer anything. The audience remained good-natured and peppy through one of the most problem-plagued opening nights in the history of theater. The first act alone ran an interminable two hours and 45 minutes, and the final curtain didn't fall till two a.m. *Variety* noted the "rough state" of the opening, but like the audience, took it in good humor:

> White himself was the star of the getaway performance. He was on the stage more than any member of the cast. When a showgal failed to appear in the opening blossoms of a rosebud because she put on the wrong costume, it opened, anyway — to reveal White inside of it. When another gal was missing in the

finale, White grabbed a hat and took her place....He never hesitated to walk out and order a number done over, showing the cast how to do it, or come out and explain away mishaps.

....On the comedy end, it's the Three Stooges who stand out. Given a load of original material, they make the best of it. One of their scenes is a Hollywood set and is supposed to show how the stand-in does all the dirty work and the star gets all the credits. Curly Howard is the stand-in, his duties consisting of absorbing three pies full in the face. Basic slapstick, it's a laugh-getter.

Larry, Moe, and Curly, circa 1940.

It was rough, but it was a diamond-in-the-rough. Top billed were vaude laugh-getters Willie and Eugene Howard — no relation to "our" Howards, but very funny men who had soared to stardom in the *Scandals of 1926*. Ben Blue, the dancer, and the song-belting Ella Logan kept up the musical end. And a 16-year-old dancer named Ann Miller stole everyone's hearts.

By the time the show hit Boston for its second "trial run,"

the show had a professional polish to match its talent. And the Stooges were again winning warm notices in the press. Elliott Norton of the *New York Times* sent this dispatch from Boston:

> The comedy reaches its high point with a topical song by Willie Howard and the Three Stooges, who are dressed in dog skins and held in leash by pretty girls for the occasion. The dogs lament that the law now keeps them in leash and restrains their street or lamp-post festivities.

Curtain calls from *George White's Scandals of 1939.*
Photo by George Karger (from the Billy Rose Collection, New York Public Library)

Some of you may have heard the phrase, "Banned in Boston," and this show almost was. After opening night, John J. Spencer, the city censor, got together with Mr. White, and several scenes were deleted. The raunchiness of some of the acts even raised a few eyebrows in jaded Manhattan. Warned the *New Yorker*: "The best advice I can give you about the *Scandals,* in fact, is that it is not the place to take a lady who has led an even moderately sheltered life."

139

(l. to r.) Sidney Salkow (director), Joan Merrill (actress), Moe Howard, Larry Fine, Curly Howard, unknown man, Anne Miller (actress), Cornelius "Connie Mack" McGillicuddy (owner of the Philadelphia A's baseball team), Glen Gray (band leader), Rudy Vallee (actor), and Allen Jenkins (actor); cast & crew from *Time Out for Rhythm* (1941). (from the collection of Mark Gilman)

But throngs welcomed Mr. White and his naughty knuckle-heads to Broadway, and the show was a smash. The New York World's Fair provided a healthy contingent of mid-Westerners eager for a peek at a scandalous revue.

The show had come a long way from its chaotic Atlantic City days, but accidents still happened. Once, the stage manager forgot to put down the huge rubber mat that protected the stage from the pie-throwing contest at the end of the Stooges' "Stand-In" sketch. So when Ann Miller danced from the wings to follow the Stooges, she took a dive in the pies and nearly slid into the orchestra pit, kicking pie-goo on the instruments.

She rushed offstage very upset, and backstage the Stooges just howled: they thought it was the funniest thing they'd ever seen.

Ann Miller returned to complete her act and receive a standing ovation. The Stooges, being gentlemen, sent her flowers and congratulations for being such a fine trouper.

When it came time for the boys to return to Hollywood, the *Scandals* and the Stooges were still the toast of Broadway.

George White pleaded with Harry Cohn to release the boys from their filmmaking duties for the run of the show, but Cohn wouldn't hear of it.

It was back to the grind of the fun factory for Larry, Curly and Moe.

HOMETOWN HERO ~~~~~~~~~~~ 1942

The very first Three Stooges fan club was a tight, little outfit: hard to find, hard to join. While later clubs debated over their favorite Stooge, Larry was the winner to this one by acclamation. It never advertised, but, boy, was it enthusiastic! Mother was the boss, and the club was known as the Feinberg family.

It was pretty exclusive for a fan club, but every so often, we took on new members. Lyla met a promising fan named Nate Budnick and married him. My wife Dinah and I had a darling daughter named Sandy and more children were on the way.

Here were some of our activities as fans:

We all went to see the Stooges flicks when they came out, but no one enjoyed them more than Mother. She never tired of repeating the prophesy of the Gypsy fortune-teller that had told her of Larry's future fame.

When the feature *My Sister Eileen* was released to rave reviews and long lines at the box office, all Mother cared about was that the Three Stooges were in it. No one told her that they were only in the final scene as excavation workmen coming up through a hole in the floor.

As she watched the film, Mother's initial pleasure turned to anxiety. Near the end, she was doing a slow burn. Finally, she stormed up the aisle and demanded to speak to the manager.

"What kind of stuff are you trying to pull here, anyway? All the ads say that the Three Stooges are in this picture! I've been sitting here for two hours, and I haven't seen my Larry yet! I'm going to..."

The manager gently interrupted her tirade and pointed to the screen. The boys had emerged through the floor; Curly had delivered his line: "We must have made a wrong turn somewhere." And now the final credits were rolling.

"Mrs. Fine," said the manager. "You just missed him."

Fannie Feinberg, Larry & Morris' mother, circa 1942.

Mother was flabbergasted. The manager gave her a free pass, not only to see *My Sister Eileen* again, but for any movies in the future.

Mother used that pass with a gusto known only to Jewish mothers: "That's my son," she'd call out in the middle of Stooge flicks.

Sometimes our family fan club would become a part of the Stooges' live act.

Moe Howard used to do a bit spoofing melodramatic actors, and he'd usually use his wife's name to refer to his unseen sweetheart: "Helen! Helen! What? Not here? She promised to meet me at the old bridge at ten o'clock!"

But when Mother was in the audience, he'd substitute her name as his lady love: "With Fannie as my wife and those papers in my possession, I can laugh at the world!"

Mother glowed with appreciation.

My daughter Sandy got into the act at the age of five. She and I had box seats right alongside the stage of the Earle, and she was delighted with seeing her Uncle Larry, clownish and rowdy in the spotlight.

As the show progressed, she became a little puzzled by all the pokes and kicks her uncle was receiving. He recovered quickly, though, and didn't seem to mind, so she let it go. But when that cad, Moe Howard, stuck his finger up Larry's nose and led her screaming uncle around the stage for what seemed like hours, her gaiety made a fast switch to concern.

"You're hurting my Uncle Larry! You're hurting my Uncle Larry!" she screamed, piercing the laughter of the crowd.

Larry immediately cut off his act and came over to our box to assure her, in full view of his bemused audience, that it was only make-believe, that he was only pretending to be in pain.

A smile peeked out through Sandy's tears: "Are you really OK, Uncle Larry?"

"You bet," he winked.

When he went back to center stage, the audience laughed and cheered. Even Moe was so cracked up that he could hardly continue.

I had been going to the fights with my brother Larry since we were kids. Now I went to the fights as a special pal of the world-famous Three Stooges.

Moe, Curly, and Larry with Larry Herman and his family of the R.E. Snider Theaters of Boston, on the set of *Time Out for Rhythm* (1941). The Stooges often posed for stills with bookers from theater chains and other movie business dignitaries.
(from the collection of Steve Cox)

Lyla's husband Nate, the Stooges and I all had ringside seats to see Johnny Forte slug it out at the arena one night, and we kicked off the evening with dinner at Lew Tendler's place. Lew's was the sporting fraternity hangout, and its assortment of fighters, managers and gamblers could have fueled scores of Damon Runyon stories.

On our way out to the arena, a friendly cry cut through the night air: "Larry, you old son of a gun! So they let you out of Hollywood!"

It was one of Larry's old school-chums, Sam Polen, and they embraced as the long-lost pals they were.

It turned out that Sam was going to the fights too. I could tell they had a lot of old times to hash over. And, faithful brother that I was, I offered to trade seats with Sam, so he could sit with Larry.

It wasn't such a bad deal: I had a great view of the ring, and the fellow next to me was someone I knew from around town. We yelled our heads off through the preliminary bouts, and at intermission, my friend left to grab a beer. When he came back, he was even more excited than he'd been during the fights.

"You should see what's going on at ringside!" he shouted. "The Three Stooges are down there, and Pat from Pat's Steaks is taking pictures with them!"

Pat Oliverri, the Steak Sandwich King, founder of a small chain of famous steak shops, was a real camera bug. He had thousands of photos with celebrities and never missed a chance for more. You can still see many of them at Pat's in Philadelphia, a great place to eat a steak sandwich.

"Hey, let's go see!" I said and allowed myself to be led to the hubbub below.

You can imagine my friend's shock when Larry spotted me and called out, "Hey, Moe, come on down here and get in on some of these pictures!"

I left my friend watching in open-mouthed amazement while I clowned around for some photos.

The fan club known as the Feinberg family was a special one indeed. How many others gave you a chance to be one of the stars?

Larry, Moe, unknown man, Shemp, and flammable birthday cake.

HOLLYWOOD HOMEOWNERS 〰〰〰〰〰 *1943*

Larry always seemed to be at loggerheads with history, the David against the Goliath of his times. When America was marching off to World War I, he was singing and dancing on the fringes of vaudeville. When the whole world seemed to be wondering where the next meal was coming from during the great Depression, Larry was living it up in palatial hotels from coast to coast. Now that the Second World War was dislocating and splitting so many families, it shouldn't surprise anyone that Larry's was consolidated as never before.

All the hotels in Atlantic City were taken over by the government as a rest and recreation center for the wounded and battle-weary. It was a warm gesture on Uncle Sam's part: going from the front or even a barrack to the President Hotel must have been quite a contrast for our boys. But it was no longer possible for the Fines to maintain their notion of being residents of Atlantic City.

At last, they were a single city household in Hollywood's Knickerbocker Hotel — earthquakes or no earthquakes. It was, of course, familiar ground by now, and Mabel had grown to like and trust the mercurial Western edge of the country. They decided to buy a house to seal their residence in California.

Producer Fred Stone had just the place: the large Mediterranean residence in the Los Feliz area of Hollywood, where he had raised his family. Paula Stone, Fred's daughter would tell Larry that the happiest years of her life were spent there.

And so it was to be for the Fines.

Moe, Curly, & Larry ready to do the "Majaraja" or "Ma-Ha Ah-Ha" routine, which they performed on stage and in *Three Little Pirates* (1946)

Larry and Mabel in front of their home in the Los Feliz section of Los Angeles.

Larry as he looked in *Idle Roomers* (1944).
(from the collection of Steve Cox)

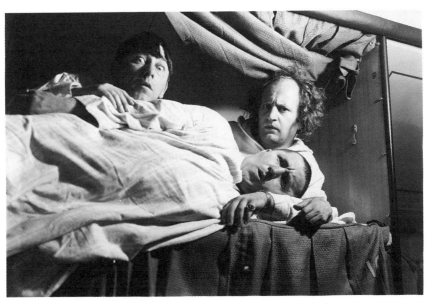

Moe, Larry, and Curly hear strange noises while trying to sleep in an upper berth.
From *A Pain in the Pullman* (1936)

The Three Stooges had branded their image on the American psyche as firmly as any vaude team in history: there was the fuzzy-head, the mop-head and the knuckle-head, doing comedy bits that seemed as ancient as the first guffaw. And the crowds were still eating it up.

It seemed unthinkable for the image to change, for a "different" Three Stooges to emerge. But reality has a way around the limits of thought: it simply happens.

In this case, it happened tragically.

Curly wasn't well. It wasn't just that he was having a hard time remembering lines. He had always had trouble with that. Some of his most inspired bits — the "nyuck, nyuck, nyuck," the "woo, woo, woo," the dramatic spins on the stage — had begun as ad-libbed covers for blown lines. He'd been like the "absent-minded professor": able to invent what no

Shemp Howard.
(from the collection of Steve Cox)

148

one else could invent, but helpless when doing what anyone could do. But now, he needed coaching on his own inventions. Too often, he seemed totally unable to concentrate on his work.

Moe blamed it on too much fast living. Larry figured it for a broken heart: Curly had one marriage annulled in his teens and was in the middle of his second divorce. In those days, that was a pretty bad score.

They found out what was happening to their unhappy cohort while filming *Half-Wits' Holiday.* It was time for Curly to rise from his chair to do one of the final scenes, and he couldn't do it. He couldn't even talk. He'd had a stroke.

Apparently, as a major earthquake can be preceded by tremors, Curly had been suffering from a series of smaller strokes, warning flashes that had gone unheeded.

Now he had no choice: it had to be treated. He had to retire from the act.

Shemp had pursued a lucrative career of his own since he'd bid the boys adieu while rehearsing for the *Passing Show of 1932.* After scoring as fight manager Knobby Walsh in Vitaphone's "Joe Palooka" shorts, he went on to simultaneous contracts with Universal and Columbia. For Universal, he appeared in features with such favorites as Abbott and Costello, the Andrews Sisters and the Dead End Kids. And for Columbia, he made "Shemp Howard" shorts. By the mid-forties, though, his contract with Universal had lapsed, and he was a wholly-owned subsidiary of Columbia. A recent short was *A Hit With A Miss,* a remake of the Stooges' *Punch Drunks* with Shemp as Curly's character.

"You ain't gonna take some nobody out of nowhere, shave his head, and tell me: 'Here's your replacement for Curly.' No one can replace Curly. We need a new character, and Shemp's the only one who knows the act!"

Moe Howard had never really hollered before at a tableful of executives, each capable of firing him. He kind of liked the feeling it produced. It made him want to go out and kick an elephant.

"Sorry, Moe," said a shaking head. "He looks too much like you."

This nastily done still originally featured Curly, not Shemp. It was used on a "Wanted for Vagrancy" poster in *Phony Express* (1943). Shemp's face was pasted over Curly's when this short was reworked to become *Merry Mavericks* (1951).
(from the collection of Joe Wallison) © 1984 Columbia Pictures Industries, Inc.

"What difference does it make?" screamed Moe. "No Shemp: no more. It's as simple as that."

So Shemp Howard became the third Stooge, as he once was, as if he always was. Now it was the fuzzy-head, the mop-head and the muddle-head, and it worked just the same.

Curly appeared in one more Stooge flick: *Hold That Lion*. It's the only film that features all four of the original "Three Stooges." Curly's the guy with the long hair and the clothes-pin on his nose, asleep on the train.

Two weeks after the release of *Hold That Lion,* on July 31, 1947, he was married to Valeria Newman. And this time, the marriage stuck. He only had five more years to live, but I like to think that, despite his illness, they were the happiest years of his life.

STUDIO SAGAS

"The Three Stooges weren't worth a damn without Larry," says Ed Bernds, one of Larry's favorite Stooge-directors.

Bernds enjoyed working with Larry's capable colleagues as well. Who could quarrel with Moe's disciplined approach to muscular humor or Shemp's wide range of character-acting skills? But Bernds saw a touch of magic in the Stooges that went beyond these areas of professional expertise, that gave them a "staying power" more prestigious comics found elusive. Bernds theorized that the magic came from the man in the middle, the least-noticed one: Larry Fine.

"I help write all our stories; all three of us do," Larry would tell me. "We're in on every story conference."

Bernds tried to give Larry more to do, to test his theory, but Larry's suggestions were usually too "off-beat" for Moe. The magic went untested.

One thing that was special about all three of the boys was their mastery of the ad lib.

"If we started to ad lib, the director let it go," Larry said. "He'd say to the cameraman, 'Just keep shooting.' They could always cut it out if it wasn't funny. Most of the time, it turned out to be funnier than what was written down. You know, it's like after something happens, you say, 'I should have said so-and-so.' Well, that's the way it happened with us. When we started doing the scene, somebody thought of something that would be funnier, and we did it. And if it turned out to be funnier, we left it in."

Larry could be a bit of a *kvetch* about scenes that struck him as dangerous, but Ed Bernds, for one, took it in stride: "Sometimes he'd complain about a gag beforehand, but once it was shot, for better or worse, he wouldn't say a word. Now, the bases of breakaway bottles can hurt, and once, Larry got a nasty cut high on his forehead. Without a complaint, he got it taped and made up and went right on shooting."

Special effects man Ray Hunt took a more jaundiced view of Larry's *kvetching*.

Ed Bernds likes to tell this story about Larry and Ray: "Once we had Larry hoisted on wires in front of a process screen. Larry was the lightest, so he was rigged above the others. He complained about the distance to the floor, and it was agreed to have him lowered when the take was going. Well, of course, he wound up on the top again. When Larry started to rag Ray about the wire snafu, he told Larry, 'Look, I never dropped an actor yet, but if you don't shut up...'"

The most important actor in most Stooges films, besides the Stooges themselves, was the sharp-nosed, wide-eyed Emil Sitka. He looked like a skinny owl. His presence was such a mainstay of the operation that many thought of him as an undeclared "fourth Stooge."

To Emil, a non-betting sports fan, the most striking thing about Larry was his gambling. His favorite "Larry story," in fact, concerns the time Emil "got suckered into betting" against our hero. The story goes pretty much like this:

Ray Hunt had a problem with one of Emil's scenes in *Fuelin' Around.* "Too tricky," he said. "It'll take all afternoon."

"Wanna bet?" said Emil, the mad Professor in the film.

The phrase, "wanna bet," always brought Larry to complete attention. After Emil sailed effortlessly through the scene, Larry turned to his stand-in, Charlie Cross, and laughed: "Leave it to Emil! When he makes a bet, he does it in one take."

"I never lose a bet," said Emil, "when I feel in my gut I can do it."

Those were gambling words to Larry, and the fight was on. Emil and Larry bet on the fights: Emil won. They bet on a baseball game: Emil won again. Finally, they got in their cars and raced from Columbia's Burbank Ranch to the Hollyood office lot on Gower. When Larry pulled across the finish line, Emil was standing by his car, reading a newspaper.

"Never bet against Emil," Larry warned colleagues after that. "He always wins."

All this begs our original question: what was so special about Larry? Perhaps it was as simple as who he was. When you think of the Three Stooges, what do you think of? Shrewd businessmen like Moe? Established character actors like Shemp? Or do you think of carefree jokers, living for the next laugh?

Perhaps it was how easy he made it look, as if anyone could do it, as if everyone were doing it, as if we were all Stooges in the too-short flick of life.

Lew Tendler in front of his famous restaurant, circa 1944.
(from the collection of the Free Library of Philadelphia: Arthur Soll, Research Photographer.)

Curly, Pat Olivieri, Mable Fine, and Larry Fine.
(from the collection of Pat's Steaks & Frank Olivieri)

(top to bottom) Curly, Moe, and Larry on Columbia's backlot, probably on a break shooting *Ants in the Pantry* (1936). (from the collection of Steve Cox)

Ed Bernds on the set of *The New Three Stooges Cartoon* (1965).

154

No one loved the Fines' spacious home in Los Feliz more than little Johnny. He could race around the yard, yell at the top of his lungs in the living room and bounce his basketball off his bedroom wall without disturbing the other guests: there were no other guests. It was their house, and they could do whatever they wanted.

Phyllis had been well into her teens when they'd bought the place and was more suspicious. "What was wrong with the Knickerbocker?" she demanded. "Why do we need a place of our own anyway?"

Mabel would smile and assure her: "We'll need all this room when you have kids of your own and bring them to visit."

Phyllis's response was the heavenward gaze and special sigh of exasperation that teenaged girls have always reserved for their mothers.

But Mabel was right: in a few short years, Phyllis was moving out to marry sportscaster Don Lamond and begin a family of her own.

Larry was delighted with his new son-in-law and pressed him regularly for "hot tips" on upcoming sports events. Whenever he was contemplating a bet, it was always "Don says this," or "Don says that."

We Jews have a word for the pride and contentment we get from our children: *naches*. It's *naches* they bring us when they go out to the wide world and become doctors, lawyers or movie stars. But nothing gives us greater *naches* than when they bring us grandchildren.

When Phyllis gave birth to Eric Lamond in 1949, Larry was so high on *naches*, you could have used him for a weather balloon.

They say it's the grandparents' perogative to spoil their grandchildren, and Larry fit the role perfectly. Nothing pleased him more than lavishing gifts upon his nearest and dearest. Mabel could hardly send him to the corner store for a cantaloupe without his returning with a new mink stole for her wardrobe.

"Who needs a baby shower with Larry as the proud grandfather?" Phyllis would say with a laugh.

The walls of Larry and Mabel's dream house resounded with the squawks and laughter of their dream.

Mabel Fine at home, 1957.

Mabel Fine on the beach at Atlantic City, New Jersey.

Larry with his grandchildren Kris and Eric Lamond at the Farmer's Market, 1957.

Just as Larry was filled with the joy of holding his first grandson, the showbiz world was cradling an infant medium that was to change the world. The name of the young whippersnapper was television.

When radio was king of home entertainment, it seemed that everyone in show business was a "star of stage, screen and radio." Not the Three Stooges: they were "Hollywood's stars of slapstick," but not of radio. Pie fights are no fun to listen to — you have to see 'em to believe 'em. Aside from occasional publicity interviews, they avoided the blind medium as irrelevant to their act.

Television, though, was another matter, and they quickly seized the chance to come bounding into the nation's living rooms. It was "Mister Television" himself — Milton Berle, or "Uncle Miltie," as he was known to the first wave of TV viewers — that first brought our sight-gag saps to the electronic screen in 1948.

Larry was a little alarmed at the frantic process of getting a live production on the air and especially at the lack of rehearsal time. But by the early fifties, they were appearing in a full range of successful shows: the *Ed Wynn Show*, the *Kate Smith Hour*, the *Colgate Comedy Hour* with Jack Paar and the *Frank Sinatra Show*.

Far from being a rocking-chair recluse, resting on his laurels, Grandpa Larry was rocketing into the second half of the century in a format straight from the pages of science fiction.

Larry and Mabel Fine with Emil Sitka on location in Newport Beach. That's Moe Howard on the boat in the background. (from the collection of Emil Sitka.)

157

Larry, Moe, and Shemp with one of their many Exhibitor's Laurel Awards.

Longtime Stooges' associate Emil Sitka in front of the marquee for the premiere of Mark Gilman's *The Funniest Guys in the World: 50 Years with The Three Stooges.* (Photo by Ann Summa, from the collection of Emil Sitka.)

Larry, Moe, Emil Sitka, and Shemp in *Pest Man Wins* (1951).

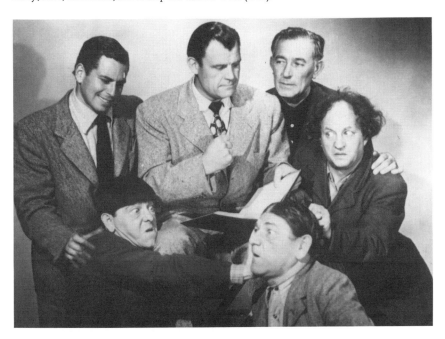

(foreground) Moe, Shemp, and Larry.
(background) Bernard Glasser (producer), Edward Bernds (director), and Paul Ivano (cameraman), in a public relations still for *Gold Raiders* (1951).

Joe Besser, Moe, and Larry from *The Three Stooges Fun-O-Rama*.
(from the collection of Mark Gilman) © 1984 Columbia Pictures Industries, Inc.

Larry, Moe, and Curly in a photo from *Uncivil Warriors* (1935) autographed to
Larry's niece Sandy, my daughter.
(from the collection of Mark Gilman)

TV YEARS

Ever since Thomas Edison first enlivened his kineto-
scope with a film of a friend sneezing in 1894, the comedy
short had been a mainstay of the movie industry. Chaplin,
Keaton, the Keystone Kops, Laurel and Hardy, a generation
of comic geniuses had forged the form into an art as rich and
uniquely American as the blues. In the early fifties, the Three
Stooges emerged as the keepers of the flame, the last of the old
masters still cranking out those eight films a year.

They won the annual Motion Picture Exhibitors' Laurel
Award for top-grossing shorts in 1950, '51, '53, '54, and '55.
They had such a commanding grip on it that some in the
industry took to calling it the "Stooge Award."

But on the night of November 23, 1955, Shemp Howard
suffered a massive heart attack on his way home from a night
at the fights. He died instantly. The act was shattered.

The boys had just finished their fourth film of the year, a
spry detective spoof called *For Crimin' Out Loud,* and had
four more to go to satisfy their contract. But what were these
films to be? Three Stooges films? What Three Stooges? Larry,
in fact, suggested they continue as the "Two Stooges": it was
the kind of Larry Fine brainstorm that Moe would have dismissed as too far-fetched in happier times. Now he blandly
passed the notion on to the executives at Columbia. The Two
Stooges. Why not? Who cared? Moe hadn't fully recovered
from Curly's death in 1952; Shemp's death devastated him.

Columbia refused to go along with Larry's scheme, and
after a few weeks of mourning, Moe was ready to tackle the
task of finding a replacement for the Stooge that had started
it all. As it happened, the solution was close at hand: Shemp's
good friend, comedian Joe Besser. Joe and Shemp had
worked together on the ill-fated *Passing Show of 1932* and the
popular 1949 Abbott and Costello flick, *Africa Screams.* He
had also proved to be an engaging stooge for the Healyesque
Milton Berle on Berle's TV show. The business end looked
simple enough: Joe was already under contract to Columbia.
So for their new 1956 contract, they were to become a threesome: Larry, Moe and Joe.

163

Publicity photo of Joe DeRita autographed to Morris "Moe" Feinberg.
(©1984 Columbia Pictures Industries, Inc.)

But Joe's contract as a Stooge didn't cover the four films still to be shot on the boys' 1955 contract: Larry and Moe had to cover those on their own. In a sense, they wound up adopting Larry's idea after all, using Shemp's double Joe Palma and lots of stock footage from previous shorts to create the illusion of a trio.

When Joe was finally available to work with Larry and Moe, his youthful pep surged through the act like Geritol. Like Curly, Joe the Stooge focused on a single, well-defined character: the aging fat boy who never grew up. While a snarling Moe was menacing a wincing Larry, Joe would transcend the entire scene with an invulnerable grin.

But there were to be no more Laurel Awards, no more offers from TV. Even the stage was suddenly innocent of Stooge-foolishness. The new Stooges were strictly a movie partnership: 1956 marked their first year without a live appearance since 1934.

There was a new edge of worry to Larry's voice when he'd call, but he'd always keep it safely grounded in a joke. "You wanna know how I'm doin'?" he said once. "I'll tell ya how I'm doing: I dropped by the set of *Father Knows Best* the other day and ran into Robert Young, who I've known since... God, it must have been Ted Healy who first introduced me to him. Anyway, he turned and started to introduce me to his leading lady. But you know me: my mouth just isn't complete unless it's gnawing on my foot. I said, 'Oh, I know Jane Wyman very well.'"

"So?" I asked.

"So it wasn't Jane Wyman! It was Jane Wyatt, different as night and day! It's a good thing it wasn't the other way around: Jane Wyman would've had me shot on the spot. As it was, I turned so red I thought they were going to sell my head for a ruby. I've been hiding out ever since: making Stooge flicks and going to bed early.

Even Larry's phone calls started to dwindle: it was six months till I heard from him again, and this time his worries were outweighing the jokes.

"Remember the Paramount, Moe?" he asked. "We played there back in nineteen who-knows-when: it was our first Howard, Fine and Howard show. Boy, we were so excited the Maxwell House people wanted to buy our blood so they could add it to their coffee."

"Yeah, yeah. The Paramount," I said, as if I'd been there. "What's up?"

"We're playing there again this Saturday: we've been rehearsing our butts off."

"Great!" I said. "When are you coming out to play the Pier again? We've missed you guys something awful."

Larry's voice slid deeper into melancholy: "O, I don't know. Call it an old gambler's hunch if you want. But we started at the Paramount, and now, I think, we're ending at the Paramount."

The phone company must have made a bundle out of the silence that followed. I was stunned beyond words. I felt as if I were witnessing the demolition of Mt. Rushmore.

It was Larry, voice breaking, that finished the thought: "I think we're through, Moe," he said.

There had been no formal announcement, but everyone at Columbia seemed to "know" that the entire Shorts Department was due to join the mastodons of the nearby La Brea tar pits in their eternal dance of extinction.

Larry had one last ace-in-the-hole, and he decided to play it. He placed a call to New York, to his sister-in-law Rose's ex-husband, the Stooges' one-time agent: Harry Romm.

Harry had done pretty well for himself since his old talent agency days. He had gone out to California, gotten involved in movie production (nothing special: a few B-movies), and had developed a tight relationship with Columbia mogul Harry Cohn. Cohn had annointed him Vice-President In Charge Of Keeping An Eye On The Big Money Boys At The Home Office and sent him back to New York. Larry figured him for a "friend in high places."

"So, what's your beef?" Harry wanted to know. "You thought maybe you had some sort of steady job?"

Good old Harry, always the joker. But good old Larry was silent as an iceberg on the other side of the line. Apparently, Larry, for all his frivolity, was one of those guys who took nearly a quarter-century with a single employer as a serious investment of time. Harry switched his tone.

"Listen, Larry," he said. "There's nothing I can do. There's nothing Cohn can do anymore. It's the accountants that run this company now. Can you imagine what would happen if... Listen, let's just keep this between us, OK? Harry's a sick man. He'll never admit it, not even to himself, but he's not the same guy who used to drop in on your set to make sure you were running on time. He's gotta separate himself, Larry."

"But Columbia began with the Shorts Department..."

"Alright, Larry, what would you do? Harry Cohn could pick up the phone tomorrow and keep you guys on the payroll from now till doomsday. But so what? The headlines alone would squelch the whole deal: 'Sentimental Mogul Bucks

Money-Tenders.' The stock would plummet, and you'd still be on the street. We'd all be on the street."

"Well, at least we'd have some company," said Larry.

A hearty laugh zipped across the continent at the speed of light. "Listen, even if they do shut down your department — and let me emphasize that no final decision has been made — but even if they do: hang in there, old buddy. We'll make money off each other yet: I can guarantee you that."

"Thanks, Harry," said Larry as he hung up the phone.

On December 20, 1957, the Three Stooges completed their last short, *Sappy Bullfighters,* and the Shorts Department was no more.

But it was hard to see how The Stooges could avoid retirement. They'd been tainted with that most gruesome of Hollywood labels: "washed up." In the fast-paced world of the overnight star, they were as invisible as the memory of a wildly alcoholic party. They were the fossils of yesteryear, and nothing more symbolized the passing of their entire era than the death of their one-time boss, Harry Cohn.

Cohn and his wife had been vacationing at the Biltmore Hotel in Phoenix with Mr. and Mrs. Harry Romm.

"Harry, I don't feel too good," Cohn said to Romm over dinner on the evening of February 26, 1958. An hour later, he was dead of a heart attack at St. Joseph Hospital.

Cohn had clearly stipulated in his will that there be no ceremony to mark his demise. But a few days later, Hollywood was treated to the spectacle of the full muscle of Cohn's company disobeying him with a vengeance: two Columbia soundstages formed the setting for one of the most extravagant funerals in history. Reporters scoured the crowd for quotes like ants at a picnic:

"He was a son of a bitch," said John Wayne.

"He was a Jekyll/Hyde type guy," said Moe Howard. "Socially, he could be very charming."

"Without Mr. Cohn," said Larry Fine, "Hollywood isn't Hollywood anymore."

"This ain't the first time we've been without a movie contract," said Larry to Moe as they left the studio.

"Yeah," snapped Moe. "There was that week we left MGM 23 years ago. Seems like only yesterday."

"Well, we can still perform," said Larry. "It's not the end of the world."

But Joe Besser wasn't about to go traipsing off in a vaudeville caravan. His wife, Ernie, had suffered a heart attack in October, and while she was recuperating nicely — a result, perhaps, of her career as a dancer — Joe was content to concentrate on his many offers near home in Los Angeles. He wound up signing with Twentieth Century Fox.

"OK, OK!" said Larry to himself. "Maybe it *is* the end of the world!"

Larry and Mabel decided to sell their home in Los Feliz. Moe Howard was prepared for anything, even retirement: he had invested wisely in the stock market. Larry had invested in the racetrack: he was prepared to move back to Philadelphia and manage apartments for a living.

Actually, I never thought of either one of the boys as retirement material. Moe was the guy who loved to regale us all with stories about his kid act on a Mississippi riverboat at the turn of the century, the guy who kept the Howard, Fine and Howard act together during their fight with Healy. A guy like that doesn't just say, "Thank you very much, Ladies and Gents; think I'll go play shuffleboard for the rest of my life."

STOOGES REDUX ～～～～～～～～～～ *1958*

"You've got to stop mourning the Three Stooges," Mabel told Larry one night. "Brooding doesn't become you."

"I'm 55 years old, for Christ's sake," Larry snapped. "You want I should get out my violin and audition for the Philharmonic?"

"Sure, if that's what you want," Mabel smiled. "You know what you need?"

Larry rested his arms on Mabel's shoulders and returned her grin: "What do I need?" He could tell it was going to be something good.

"A week in Vegas, just the two of us. Forget about your career for a while. It'll come back to you, if you let it."

Moe's investments might have won the retirement sweepstakes, but Larry wasn't exactly donning dark glasses and selling pencils on Sunset Boulevard. They could afford a little trip to Vegas, if Larry behaved himself.

THE THREE STOOGES, "Clown Princes" of Comedy
Monday, Tuesday, Wednesday, Thursday, Friday 5:45 to 6:30, Saturday to 5:30 p.m.
ON KPLR-TV-CHANNEL 11

Handout for The Three Stooges shorts show on KPLR-TV
(Channel 11).
(from the collection of Jeff & Greg Lenburg)

A few days later, a revitalized Larry Fine was placing a
long distance call from Las Vegas to Moe Howard in Hollywood. He had "the find of a lifetime" to share.

"I know what your big discovery is, Porcupine," growled
Moe. "You're broke, right?"

Larry hardly heard him: "You remember Joe DeRita, don't
you?"

"Burlesque comic? Little fat guy? Sure."

Their paths had crossed fairly frequently over the years.
Joe DeRita had made a few shorts for Columbia in the late
forties. On the road, DeRita played the burlesque houses
while the Stooges played the vaudeville circuit. Whenever
they played the same town, Larry would get together with
him and swap jokes.

"Mabel and I caught his act at the Dunes Hotel last night,"
said Larry. "He's in Harold Minsky's *Follies Of 1958,* and
he's a scream. He's Curly, Lou Costello and the fat lady at the
opera all rolled into one. I'll tell ya, Moe: he'd be perfect for the
third Stooge."

It was standard practice for Moe to approach Larry's ideas with a certain wariness, and Larry's extravagant enthusiasm just deepened Moe's suspicion. "You say he's in Minsky's *Follies*. How do you know he's even available?"

"Would I be calling you if he wasn't? He's leaving the show next week and coming out to L.A. to do a movie. It's a one-shot deal; shouldn't be a conflict. You can check him out then."

But Joe DeRita proved hard to pin down. Almost immediately upon arriving in Los Angeles, he was off to Mexico for four weeks of shooting on location: playing the part of the hangman in Henry King's Twentieth Century Fox film, *The Bravados*. When he returned to Hollywood, it was for a frenzied string of TV appearances: *Desilu Playhouse, This Is Alice, Bachelor Father....*

It wasn't till July, four months after Larry had spotted him in Las Vegas, that the boys could give DeRita a serious tryout. To Moe's surprise, the audition went well: Larry's suggestion hadn't been half bad. De Rita certainly looked the part of a Stooge. He was five feet, three inches tall, about the same as Larry and Moe, and his 225 pounds automatically gave him the look of a human cartoon. With his hair neatly combed he was reminiscent of Joe Besser's angelic patsy; when he parted it shaggily down the middle, he evoked Shemp's unsavory bum.

For a Stooge, DeRita's comic style was remarkably passive, even genteel — a sharp contrast to the knockabout chaos Larry and Moe had made famous. But civility was clearly the wave of the future as far as the Stooges were concerned. Joe Besser had even written a provision into his contract that forbade Moe from hitting him. Joe DeRita might have been mild-mannered, but at least he could take a slap or two.

Moe decided to give him a try before a live audience. He arranged for the three of them to do a free gig at Camp Pendleton in Riverside, California. The comedy-starved G.I.s ate it up, and Moe was convinced: Joe DeRita was the new third Stooge.

Their next performance was something of a letdown. It was a professional booking at Martin Jiosa's, a nightclub in Bakersfield.

"We bombed so bad they didn't even throw tomatoes,"

Larry, Moe, and Curly-Joe, in a give-away promotional photo.

Larry said later. "It was really pathetic. The management almost didn't pay us."

Moe was having second thoughts about Joe DeRita and the whole process of staging a comeback. There was such a long way to go, and suddenly it seemed too ludicrous: three tired, old clowns, fallen from stardom, failing at an entry-level gig. Perhaps, like boxers and baseball players, physical comedians were meant to retire early.

Larry did his best to be the ever-buoyant cheerleader against Moe's gloom, but gloom can be fiercely contagious. Gloom is the emotion of seriousness, and seriousness is the texture of reason. Larry was in need of a few hard facts to support his gusto, his belief that there was still an audience out there. How the Stooges found that audience and who they were was nothing short of a show-business phenomenon.

Columbia had released 78 old Stooges shorts to television as a marketing experiment, and, to everyone's surprise, they were a smash hit: number one in the ratings for the after-school time-slot nearly everywhere they were picked up. But that merely served to enliven Moe's mood with anger. In those

171

Moe, Larry, & Curly-Joe.

days, you didn't get residuals when they showed your old movies on TV. Even when Ronald Reagan's Screen Actors Guild finally forced the studios to pay TV residuals, the deal only covered movies made after 1959. The Stooges were getting good ratings, but ratings didn't pay the rent. Moe felt robbed.

It was a phone call from Lyla that put things in perspective: "Do you have any idea what's happening out here, Larry? You guys are such stars, it's ridiculous. Every kid in the neighborhood wants your autographed picture. They even want my autograph!"

"Well, it sure ain't happening here," said Larry. "The crowds we get these days, you can't get so much as a pulse out of 'em."

"Where have you played? Bakersfield? Do they have TV yet in Bakersfield?"

"Well, they aren't playing our movies. That's for sure."

"Wait till you come out here, Larry. All you'll have to do is sign autographs. That's all they want. These kids love you."

"Throw a roast in the oven," Larry exulted. "We'll be right over."

Larry and the boys didn't make it back East quite that fast, but by the end of the year, they were in Pittsburg for the show that would change everything. A one-week booking at a nightclub called the Holiday House produced such a flood of happy children that they had to add afternoon matinees and extend their run to a full three weeks. Nine hundred kids turned out for each show, packed into a room built for seven hundred. The manager was so elated that he took the unusual step of taking out an ad in *Variety* to express his gratitude to our boys. It included this open letter:

> Dear Moe, Larry and Joe:
>
> We are just now recovering from your sensational record breaking three-week engagement at the Holiday House (Dec. 22 to Jan. 10), and I would like to take this opportunity to thank you for your unstinted cooperation in writing a new page in Pittsburgh nightclub history.
>
> You have made thousands of new friends among the small fry and the adults too, for yourselves and for the Holiday House, and you have done an outstanding job for me. I'm sure it must have been gratifying to you to play to capacity crowds for every show, and to have been received so enthusiastically.
>
> My very best wishes for your continued success. We are looking forward to your return visit.
>
> Cordially and Appreciatively,
> Johnny Bertera

Like the phoenix rising from the ashes, the Three Stooges were born again.

"OK, boys and girls, raise your hands up high and repeat after me: 'I promise not to imitate the Three Stooges.'"

Those words, telecast in 1959 by Philadelphia's TV cowgirl, Sally Starr, should just be now reaching whatever planetary system may exist around the star, Betelgeuse, 26 light years away. Perhaps a chorus of antenna-headed, schmoo-like space beings are sitting at their video monitors and obediently answering, "I promise not to imitate the Three Stooges," to see what happens next.

"Now if you all said that, and you didn't have your fingers crossed," the transmission continues, "we'll watch the Three Stooges."

What would these space creatures make of the knockabout chaos to follow? How would they react? Would they imitate the Stooges after all and reach far into the black of space to give the planet Earth the old one-two slap? Should we be concerned?

In the late fifties, many parents on Earth were very concerned about the effects of this and other Stooge-casts — not on space creatures, necessarily, but on their own children. The *TV Guide* of March 21, 1959, paints the worry in all its ghoulish splendor:

> If little Crockery, who has always been a quiet child, suddenly forks his fingers into Mother's eyes, it's probably too late to do anything about it. Too bad the storm warnings never went up!

Well, the storm warnings did go up. And up. An interview with the Stooges themselves in the same article did little to defuse the issue:

> 'Don't play up that business about mothers,' Moe told a reporter menacingly.

In presenting the Stooge shorts, Sally Starr was careful to draw a line between real violence and the cartoonish deviltry of our boys. The Stooges themselves appeared on the show as the kindly grandfathers they really were. A special effects

Martha Raye delivers the dread triple slap to the triple Stooges on the Danny Thomas Special.

Larry was always the lightest of the Stooges and working with Joe DeRita didn't change anything. Here's Larry "floating" from some anti-gravity cords in *Have Rocket Will Travel* (1959).

man from the Theater Guild came on to unravel the mystery of how the Stooges could beat each other up but not get hurt. He demonstrated how to pull a fist-full of hair out by the roots: you need crack timing, a piece of sailcloth ripping next to a microphone, artificial hair and a grimace of pain.

Sally mollified the parents somewhat, and kids loved her. How could you not love someone who would ride horseback on Philadelphia's newest super-highway, the Schuylkill Expressway? But even without her, kids had the flicks pegged as unreal. Punch a Stooge, and he'd bounce right back as if nothing happened. If it was violence, it sure wasn't the grisly stuff of gangster movies or the local news: it was safe to laugh at.

In fact, casting mayhem into make-believe could sometimes have the beneficial effect of allowing kids to better accept and deal with their natural feelings of anger.

The *TV Guide* of March 6, 1965, tells this story:

> When she became upset, the emotionally disturbed 12-year-old girl spoke and wrote only in numbers. For instance, when she was angry, she cried out numbers ending in 4, the number becoming larger with the degree of her anger. Psychiatrists at Los Angeles County General Hospital called her condition a 'numbers syndrome.' Eventually they discovered that the numbers corresponded with those on Three Stooges bubble-gum trading cards, which depicted the moods of violence the girl felt but because of her emotional problems could not otherwise release.

The girl had invented her own "play therapy." It wasn't the Stooges that troubled her. Quite the contrary: it was the Dr. Howard, Dr. Fine and Dr. Howard team of old that had provided a way for her to externalize, and finally communicate, her inner conflicts.

In the 1959 *TV Guide* we examined earlier, the anthropologist Margaret Mead bemoaned the "tendency to treat all violence as identical," and pointed out that rough edges to young fantasies were often healthy:

> ....Children in particular enjoy seeing safely enacted in an unreal world dreadful deeds which they daydream about but would never dare imitate. Parents do seem like giants to children, and it's delightful to

see them bested by giant-killers, aged nine or ten....It is tiresome to have good table manners, and a glorious relief to see grown men throwing pies in each others' faces....Children even feel better, more like good children, their anger and hate drained safely out of them...

To Mead, the proper target for parental ire was violent realism — the serious stuff, not the laugh-getters.

The Stooge flicks stayed on the air, and the kids behaved themselves. No one threw pies across the table at Thanksgiving; no one poked out anyone's eyes.

But beware of flying saucers that go, "nyuck, nyuck, nyuck."

Larry, Curly-Joe, & Moe in New York.
(from the collection of Joe Wallison)

177

Don Lamond and Chrissy Lamond, Larry's son-in-law and
granddaughter, 1957.

Phyllis Fine Lamond, 1957.

I was in a limousine with the Three Stooges. It was inching its way down Philadelphia's Broad Street, which had been converted to a one-way street for the occasion. Thousands of cheering fans choked the sidewalk. Young fathers lifted their screaming youngsters to their shoulders to afford them a better view of us.

It was September 11, 1959, and the Stooges were on their way to Connie Mack Stadium for the Police and Firemen's Thrill Show, the biggest charity extravaganza of the year. The purpose of the affair was to build a Hero Scholarship Fund for the children of brave public servants who had been killed in the line of duty. Tony Bennett and Polly Bergen were slated to entice the adults. The rock 'n' rolling Bobby Rydell brought the teens, and the Three Stooges captured the kids.

This was the year of the Stooges' comeback, and it seemed to be getting more amazing by the day. They had gone over so well at Philadelphia's Latin Casino that *Time* magazine covered it as the birth of a new phenomenon: nightclub acts for children. They had returned in triumph to Atlantic City's Steel Pier, where they once again opened the summer season with yelps of joy. But the Thrill Show was something else. This was no mere comeback: the Stooges weren't just playing theatres; they were packing them in football stadiums!

As I sat in the limousine, I thought of the luncheon that the Hero Scholarship people had just hosted — a formal Society affair with such local dignitaries as Mayor Richardson Dillworth and Mrs. John B. Kelly, mother of the late Princess Grace.

"Those kids out there would never believe it," I told Larry. "There we were with the cream of society, and you guys didn't throw a single pie."

It was left to Mother Nature to lend a little chaos to the proceedings. At Connie Mack Stadium, midway through the Thrill Show, Polly Bergen was hammering home a medley of her greatest hits. Suddenly, the skies opened to unleash the Great Downpour of 1959. Everyone scurried for cover. Polly Bergen rushed off the stage — her elegant gown, a dripping

The Three Stooges on the set of *Three Stooges Scrapbook* (1960).
(from the collection of Steve Cox)

shambles — to assist wheelchair-bound members of the audience toward shelter. She was magnificent.

As people dashed for their cars, loudspeakers blared that the two remaining acts — Tony Bennett and the Three Stooges — had agreed to do a special live telecast on WFIL-TV the following evening.

The next day, Larry, Moe Howard, and I decided to take in a baseball game before reporting to the TV station.

Signs of their newfound popularity were everywhere.

We didn't have tickets for the game, so Larry tried his old trick of walking up to the press gate and telling them that we had been invited by the Phillies' management. For the first time in years, it actually worked!

The Phillies were playing the St. Louis Cardinals that day, and Moe and Larry decided to check in on some friends of theirs in the Cards' dressing room. Larry was a Philadelphia boy, but he was a star in St. Louis, too.

Solly Hemus, the Cards' manager and a former Phillies player, greeted us warmly and insisted on calling his players together to meet the Stooges.

There they were, the famous Gas House Gang, in all stages of undress: some with nothing on but a jockstrap. The whole team crowded around Larry and Moe, asking them to autograph baseballs — which appeared as if by magic. Even my idol, Stan Musial, held out a ball to my brother, the resurgent star.

We had to leave in the middle of the game to get to the TV station on time. I got the feeling that Larry's visits were going to be very fast-paced for the next few years.

WFIL had worked round the clock on no notice to telecast Tony Bennett and the Three Stooges, and the effort showed. They had a nice orchestra for Bennett and an elaborate set for the Stooges.

The Thrill Show ended on a graceful note of well-oiled professionalism as the Three Stooges nailed down their superstardom with Larry's hometown fans.

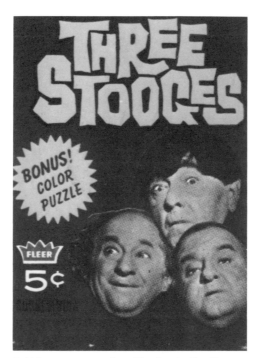

Bubble gum wrapper from Fleer's set of trading cards.

Larry was singing "Hooray For Hollywood" at the top of his lungs as he drove his shiny new Cadillac up to the apartment hotel he and Mabel called home.

It was a great time to be a Stooge. Joe DeRita had sharpened his character, gotten a close crewcut and become "Curly-Joe." The Stooges were making a new film for Columbia: a feature produced by Harry Romm and titled, *Have Rocket, Will Travel.* And the news media was going beserk over what *Time* Magazine called "the most startling comeback of many a show business season."

Larry handed the keys of his Cadillac over to the parking attendant of his building and turned to face the nervous young man who'd been pacing up and down the sidewalk.

"Are you Carl?" asked Larry. "Sorry I'm late. The traffic's as thick as the smog."

The young fellow nodding deferentially was Carl Nelson, the son of a dear friend of Mabel's. He was a budding journalist, and Mabel hoped to enhance his career by arranging an exclusive interview with Larry for him. Larry led him to their suite for a chat.

"Do you guys ever get hurt on the set?" asked our young reporter after they'd settled on Larry's couch.

"Are you kidding?" said Larry. "My lip is still all swollen from an accident we had last week on our new picture. See, we're the first people to land on the planet Venus, and we were running around in spacesuits. Joe knocked me down, and the next thing I knew, I was looking up at a doctor. My lip had been crushed between my teeth and the space helmet. They bandaged me up and adjusted the helmet so it wouldn't show. That kind of thing happens all the time. You just go back to work and don't let it bother you."

"Tell me about your family," said Carl. "I've met Mabel, but I can never keep your grandchildren straight."

"Actually I thought Mabel would be back by now. She's probably still at Johnny's place, helping out with our new granddaughter. Let's see: Johnny is 23 years old, married, with two daughters. Christy Lynne is two now, and Phyllis Lorraine is the newborn. I also have a daughter, Phyllis Lamond. She's married to Don Lamond — the guy who manages our show on KTTV, channel 11. He's also the narrator in *Have Rocket Will Travel,* by the way. Their son Eric is ten and Christy Ann is four. Eric's really following the old family tradition. He'll be appearing with us on the Frances Langford TV show and has done numerous commercials: Standard Oil, lots of others. He's a real sharp-looking kid."

"You mention the Frances Langford show. Do you have any other TV shows in the works?"

"O, sure: Steve Allen, Ed Sullivan. We get more offers than we can handle. There isn't enough violence on the tube already," Larry laughed.

"How do you respond to charges that your act is too rough?"

"I just send 'em to see Moe. He fixes 'em up. Actually, we don't do much of that stuff anymore. Columbia is sending us to finishing school in our old age."

Carl laughed and fumbled through his notes for his next question. "I'm kinda new at this," he admitted sheepishly.

"That's OK," said Larry. You could say I'm still getting used to holding up my end of conversations like this. A year ago, we couldn't get coverage in *My Weekly Reader.*"

"Well, let me get to the fan club kind of questions."

"O, like what time do I get up in the morning? Well, I watch the 'Late, Late Show.' I can sleep till noon if I have to. We sleep with the windows open. Neither of us can stand heat."

"Yeah, that's the stuff," said Carl. "Got any special phobias?"

"I'm scared of planes, but I ride 'em. I drive the seat."

"Favorite music?"

"Jazz. I like the higher class stuff like Andre Previn."

"Favorite singer?"

"O, Peggy Lee, Dinah Shore, Sinatra, Dean Martin....The Stooges did a song once with Dean Martin at a club in Philly. We were the Stinkpots: you know, like the Inkspots. That was about fifteen years ago, back before Dean got his nose job."

"Nose job? What nose job?"

"Christ, you should've seen him! He looked like Pinocchio!"

Carl shook his head and smiled: "Maybe I should talk to Dean Martin next. How about aversions; do you have any pet peeves?"

Larry shot a sly grin at the young fellow. "Long conversations," he said.

The Three Stooges had been delighted with the chance to do *Have Rocket, Will Travel.* It was a double-decker homecoming: a chance to work with their old manager Harry Romm at Columbia, the studio that had once spurned them.

But it soon became apparent that Moe and Romm had lost their easy comraderie over the years. They fought over every aspect of the production. Who knows what they fought about? Larry was having nothing to do with it.

"The only kind of fight I'll sit still for is the kind ya bet on," Larry liked to say.

The Stooges met their next producer while appearing on NBC's *Frances Langford Show,* a Mother's Day special. Charles Wick, the show's producer, liked their work and proposed a deal. He'd been searching for a project to showcase Carol Heiss, the Olympic iceskating star. Suddenly, it clicked: *Snow White and the Three Stooges.*

Twentieth-Century Fox sank 3.5 million dollars into the film, but Larry and the boys were disappointed with it. "It wasn't our style," Larry explained. "It was the most serious movie we ever made. There were a couple of scenes in there that were really sad. I don't mean sad. I mean SAD!"

The movie producer that the Stooges settled on to guide the rest of their career was Moe's son-in-law, Norman Maurer. Norman was the very model of Hollywood's new breed of producers: equally at home brainstorming gags or analyzing market research data. He was always saying things like: "Let's take a meeting on the pilot project."

Larry feigned ignorance of the new lingo. "In my day," he'd say, "I didn't 'take meetings.' I took beatings!"

Larry was a big fan of the Three Stooges comic books that Norman had been drawing since joining the Stooge family in 1947. Norman had shown a lot of business acumen in his management of various Stooge merchandizing ventures. And now he was turning out well-considered movie treatments and scripts with a passion that promised a string of successes as far as the mortal eye could see. Moe Howard had grown weary of living from movie deal to movie deal, and Norman Maurer offered the road to stability. The Three

Stooges signed a contract with Norman's Normandy Productions for films to be released by Columbia. The boys had found their niche once again.

For the boys' first Normandy Production, *The Three Stooges Meet Hercules,* Norman Maurer brought back two fave raves from the Stooges' two-reeler days: director Edward Bernds and screenwriter Elwood Ullman. It proved to be a winning combination for the ticket-takers, the audience and the critics. Here's what the *New York Times* had to say on January 27, 1962:

> ....This time the boys kid the very stuffings out of every togaed spectacle from *Ulysses* right up to *Ben Hur.* Even H.G. Wells gets his comeuppance when Larry, Moe and Curly-Joe, as pharmacy workers in Ithaca, N.Y., go sailing back to ancient Ithaca, 900 B.C., clutching a "time machine" that looks like a dismantled Model T Ford.
>
> The ensuing complications are as corny as they are funny, but anybody who doesn't chuckle at some of the bedlam should consult a Delphic Oracle....
>
> The picture...is, of course, about as subtle as a bulldozer. But credit Moe, Larry and Curly-Joe with stepping on the gas and knowing what to step on for fun if not art. Hurry back, boys, and don't forget the pies.

As good as *The Three Stooges Meet Hercules* was for the team, the time of its production was a difficult one for Larry.

First, there was the inevitable injury on the set: Larry and Curly-Joe falling out of a racing chariot with Curly-Joe landing on top. Now, a falling Curly-Joe could daze an elephant. Larry was knocked out cold and raced to the hospital.

By the time Larry was released, his doctor had a classic "good news/bad news" line for him: "Well, Mr. Fine, I can report that you'll emerge from these injuries without a scratch. But I'm afraid our tests revealed an unexpected illness: diabetes."

"Good old modern medicine," said Larry. "I didn't even feel sick, and already you have the diagnosis!"

Suddenly, the jokester who could bounce back from being told he'd just eaten a can of dog food by asking what brand it was was being put on dietary restrictions.

"So I'll be more careful. So what's the big deal?" was Larry's assessment. "They may not have a cure for it, but they have a treatment. That's good enough for me."

Larry's next setback, though, haunted him for the rest of his life: his son Johnny was killed in a car accident.

I had to communicate indirectly with him during this period. One of the ways he observed the traditional Hebrew seven-day period of mourning was by disconnecting his telephone.

The Three Stooges In Orbit followed the lead of *Hercules* in riding the boys' popularity. Here's what the July 11, 1962 issue of *Variety* had to say:

> Clonk for clonk and splat for splat, *Orbit* attains more comedy mileage than *Hercules*. Again the formula is slapstick farce in a fantasy theme, with Elwood Ullman's screenplay, from producer Norman Maurer's story, following the classic pattern of 'Stooges' comedy: three heads are better than one, if jarred together at periodic intervals.

This picture contains one of Curly-Joe's favorite ad libs. While taking a submarine-tank-helicopter for a test-flight, the Stooges are about to crash until Moe alertly pilots the craft to safety. Curly-Joe turns to Moe and says, "You're a good boy," as he plants a kiss on Moe's cheek. Moe gives Joe a very surprised look, believe me.

The Three Stooges Go Around The World In A Daze was Maurer's debut as a director. It was a send-up of Mike Todd's *Around The World In Eighty Days*, and it easily hit the standards of success to which the Stooges had happily become accustomed. "Another healthy box office entry from the durable slapstick comedy team," sang *Variety*.

Curiously, Moe Howard winced at the word, "slapstick," being applied to the Stooges. "Slapstick belongs to the wonderful clowns of the circus, not us," he'd say.

Larry and I, though, didn't follow the distinction: "Well, what are we, then?" Larry would say. "We're too dirty for vaudeville, too clean for burlesque, too ratty for Broadway. Ya gotta call us something, and you can't print the other things in the newspaper!"

Curly-Joe, Moe, and Larry as the rescue team from the United Artists' release, *It's A Mad, Mad, Mad, Mad World.*
(from the Movie Still Archive) ©1963 Casey Productions, Inc.

The Stooges even found time to pop their famous faces into Warner Brothers' *Four For Texas,* starring Sinatra's "rat pack."

They also appeared in United Artists' *It's A Mad, Mad, Mad, Mad World* which features carloads of slapstick and the longest chase in film history. At the end nearly every comic living in America is stuck on a fire escape that's about to collapse. But wait! The rescue squad is here to save the day. And as the camera pans across the fire trucks and police cars, we see Moe, Larry, and Curly-Joe dressed in rescue uniforms. They are on the screen for less than half a minute. They never move or say a word and yet, it's one of the film's guaranteed laughs. The Three Stooges' *schtick* was such an institution at this point that all they had to do in *Mad World* was appear at the scene of a disaster in firemen's suits, and people got the joke: the comics in danger were doomed.

Norman Maurer's *The Outlaws Is Coming* was the Stooges' tribute to the TV hosts who had brought them back to the attention of America's kids. Paul Shannon, who had introduced them to Pittsburgh's frenzied youngsters at the Holi-

Dean Martin with The Three Stooges in *4 For Texas*.
(from the collection of the Movie Still Archive) (The Sam Company ©1964. Courtesy Warner Bros. Inc.)

day House in 1958, was Wild Bill Hickock. Philadelphia's own Sally Starr was Belle Starr. New York City's smiling neighborhood cop, Officer Joe Bolton, turned in his badge for a stab at the role of Rob Dalton.

A special Stooge plane circled the country, picking up excited TV personalities. "I was the second to be swept away," said Sally Starr. "Joe Bolton was already aboard. We just kept hopscotching around the country. That day, I had three breakfasts, two lunches and one dinner!"

Hollywood, of course, was the strangest part of the journey. "In the movies, you just don't realize how short the Stooges are," said Officer Joe. "I was amazed. Next to Adam West, who played the cowardly sheriff, they looked like midgets."

"Larry knew that I wasn't exactly at ease on the movie set," said Sally Starr. "So, he kept telling me jokes. He had a little, white poodle that he always brought with him on the set, and he'd let me hold the poodle while he'd do his scenes. Instead of giving the dog a treat, he'd give it to me. I'd put the dog biscuit in my mouth and the poodle would take it out."

THE THREE STOOGES

Give-away card featuring the characters
from *The New Three Stooges Cartoon* (1965)
drawn by Norman Maurer.

Joe Bolton's official officer's logo.

The most dangerous part of the production was the buffalo stampede. The special effects team dug a hole in the ground for the cameramen to get a shot of the buffaloes' feet running over them. None of the cast forgot that scene: when the filming was over, Moe had everyone over to his house in the Hollywood Hills for a buffalo barbecue.

MABEL ~~~~~~~~~~~~~~~~~ 1966-1967

A Fortieth Wedding Anniversary is a rare event in show biz circles. Larry and Mabel decided to celebrate theirs in style, surrounded by the splendor of Las Vegas. The manager of the Riviera Hotel, an old friend of the two lovebirds, set them up in the most luxurious bridal suite in the place.

"I don't wanna say we had a large suite," Larry would say later, "but the Beatles dropped by to see if they could use it to stage a concert!"

The Fines were having breakfast in bed when Room Service called to announce the arrival of a Special Delivery package from Philadelphia.

"Send it on up," cried Larry with the relish of a ringmaster.

Fifteen minutes later, two bellboys eased into the room, struggling with a large television crate. Larry and Mabel exchanged puzzled looks. They knew lots of crazy people in Philadelphia, but who would send them a TV set? Their curiosity piqued, they opened it to reveal the anniversary gift that Lyla and I had sent.

It was a huge silver loving cup, made to order by a Philadelphia firm that makes trophies for sporting events. The 40-inch high cup was mounted on an elegant hardwood base. I'd put together a flower arrangement of white silk roses, fern fronds and green leaves that graced the top of the cup. I was in the display business then, and I felt really proud of the job I'd done on that loving cup.

The elegant trophy was engraved, "To Mabel and Larry Fine, winners in the Forty-Year Marriage Sweepstakes on January 22, 1966.

A plate on the base read, "From your loving family," and listed all our names. I started the list, followed by my wife Dinah, our daughters Eileen and Sandy, Sandy's husband Marvin and their daughters Robin and Joy. Of course, Lyla was included, along with her husband Nate. Concluding the list were their daughters Karen, Phyllis, Joan, Barbara and her husband Larry.

They called that day to thank us. "You know, Moe," said Larry. "I told a reporter a while back that my life's ambition was to win the Irish Sweepstakes. This is better."

Larry & Mabel Fine in one of their last photos together at Eileen Feinberg's wedding, Oct. 28, 1966.

Trophy sent to Larry and Mabel Fine by their family to mark their 40th wedding anniversary.

On October 28, 1966, our youngest daughter Eileen was getting married to her Irv. It was a tradition in our clan for the following things to happen whenever there was a wedding:

Larry and Mabel would arrive a few days early and stay at their favorite boardinghouse, Lyla and Nate's place. It was a large house, and Lyla loved playing the hostess for the throngs of friends and relatives the Fines attracted.

The wedding would take place at Uhr's Wynne. With a chapel, seven banquet halls and a reputation as Philadelphia's prime caterers, it was the perfect site.

Our wedding parties would always be augmented a bit by autograph hounds from neighboring receptions, but we'd shrug it off with good humor. We learned long ago to share our Larry with the world.

All our children's weddings were happy occasions, but I particularly cherish the memory of Eileen and Irv's. It was the last time I'd see Larry and Mabel together.

In the spring of 1967, the Three Stooges were on a tour of the Mid-Atlantic states. Lyla's husband Nate was along, acting as road manager and sound effects man, a role he'd had, off and on, for more than a decade. They were in Providence, Rhode Island on Memorial Day, and Lyla had joined them for the weekend.

Larry called Mabel every evening when he was on the road, and that night was no exception. Mabel mentioned that Phyllis had dropped by, and they were spinning schemes to take the next flight to Atlantic City for a vacation.

"Wait'll I get back," Larry laughed. "I wanna come along!"

A few minutes after they hung up, Phyllis called back: "Larry, Mabel just died!"

A heart attack had killed her instantly. Larry was in shock; he and Lyla left for Hollywood immediately.

Larry's life was never to be the same, but he did his best to bounce back: "Even the comedians that make you laugh the hardest, have tragedies in their lives," he said once. "Laughter is all we have against the pain of life and death."

Larry Fine and Morris Feinberg, circa 1960.

Larry with his niece Eileen and her husband Irv Dogon, 1968.

LEAVE 'EM LAUGHIN'

It begins with a film editor's dream: a fast-paced montage of black-and-white clips from *The Three Stooges Meet Hercules* to *The Outlaws Is Coming!* Less than five years' work is represented here, but the quick edits and wide range of gags gives us a sense of retrospective, a feeling that their whole lives in show business are passing before our eyes.

Suddenly, the film is in color, and Larry, Moe and Curly-Joe appear as "real people": in street clothes and well-mannered hair. They explain that after entertaining for more than half a century, they've never seen anything of life but the insides of their dressing rooms. It's time to see the world as it is, to explore the natural bounty of the planet. They are retiring from show business, they tell us, and setting off on a tour of our wonderful National Park system.

Cameras, of course, are permitted.

"You guys have come up with crazy ideas before, but this beats 'em all," I told Larry. "People think you're made of greasepaint. Who's gonna believe you'd ever retire from the stage?"

"We'll have to retire when they release it," Larry joked. "We didn't even use a script!"

It was true: *Kook's Tour,* shot on the road in the summer of '69, was a tour de farce of that old Stooge specialty, ad libbing. Even the business end was a gamble. It was a "made for TV" film without any prior interest or contract with any network. Norman Maurer had a promising outline; the boys had plenty of experience, and everyone had a little money to spend. So they decided to make a movie. Simple as that.

For all his kidding, Larry loved *Kook's Tour* — and why not? Larry's sterling example of how not to fish, spurred on by Moe's injunction that what "you don't catch, you don't eat," is the running gag of the film.

As the travelogue commences, we see Moe in two roles: the earnest narrator sitting at a desk in his den and offering educational insights on the areas to be visited, and the hapless Stooge directing his colleagues in the loading of the camper.

From Moe's house in the Hollywood Hills, the Stooges venture into southern Idaho where they treat us to a demonstration of things to avoid while launching an 80-pound boat on a river. As the boys stand on shore, watching their craft float away, their dog Moose jumps in the water and retrieves it. The Stooges climb aboard and sail on into the heart of laughter.

One of the highlights of the film occurs when the boys try new careers as con artists in Yellowstone National Park. Spotting some tourists, the Stooges produce a contraption of pipes and valves which they claim can control the geysers. They check their watches, turn a few handles, and presto: Old Faithful erupts! The crowd is amazed, but the far-off sirens of approaching rangers cues our boys to depart.

Larry later mentioned that the real-life park officials frowned on this sequence for fear that viewers would miss the joke and be led to believe that the Stooges were actually controlling the geysers.

In other Stooge epics, an injury or close call on the set demanded a re-take; in *Kook's Tour,* it was just another ad lib.

In one scene, Curly-Joe invents a vacuum mini-bike to clean up after litterbugs. But a real accident occurred when DeRita hit a rope on a pitched tent and fell from his bike. Not wasting the shot, producer-director Norman Maurer and his son Jeff enter the scene in camping attire and tell DeRita that he should be more careful.

Another brush with danger occurred when the Stooges were playing in paddle boats and Moe's got caught in the current. Though threatened with being swept down the river, Larry and Curly-Joe were able to rescue Moe and still make the scene play for laughs.

Laughter and terror drink from the same pool.

Kook's Tour turned out to be the last film by Larry and the boys. It shares an important feature with their first, *Soup To Nuts:* almost no one has ever seen it. *Kook's Tour* was never released, and *Soup To Nuts* has long since disappeared.

The movie career of this fabulous trio begins and ends not on the screen but in our imaginations.

Ceramic eyeglasses holder in the shape of a dog's head which Larry made and gave as gifts.

THE STROKE ∼∼∼∼∼∼∼∼∼∼∼∼∼∼∼ *1970*

It could've been midnight; it could've been three a.m. I don't remember the time, but the date is etched in my memory: January 9, 1970. Our lives would never be the same.

Phyllis called, frantic with worry: "Larry's in the hospital!"

"What happened?"

"I don't know, Moe. He can't even talk!"

"Is he going to be OK?"

"They don't know yet. His face is all twisted up..."

"Was it a heart attack? A stroke?"

We've had a history of stroke and heart attack on both sides of the family. Dad had died of a stroke, and now the villainous condition had returned.

It was a stroke.

The next few days were tough for all of us. No one was allowed to visit Larry, not even Moe Howard. Phyllis was keeping word of Larry's illness from the press to protect his privacy. We were on the phone every night with Phyllis and often with Larry's doctors trying to find out what had happened, whether he would live, and what his condition would be if he did survive.

The pain of being so far away from Larry in his time of trouble racked the family. But through the tears, over time, we pieced together the story of his illness.

This is how it happened:

For once, the weather forecasters were right, and by the time Larry got home from his ceramics class, he was soaked from head to toe. But the chill of the rain did nothing to dampen his high spirits: he'd been working with some beautiful glazes, and he was looking forward to a dinner date with Phyllis in an hour. He hummed happily to himself as he changed his clothes.

Then Mr. Fate stepped in with his one-two punch. A wave of nausea rolled over him. He thought he'd better stay home and called Phyllis to cancel dinner.

He lay down to rest, and a numbness grabbed his left leg and crept up his left side, stroking his neck with cold iron fingers. His face twisted; his mouth wrenched down. He was paralyzed: he couldn't move or speak.

Although Larry had been his usual, casually jocular self on the phone to Phyllis, something had bothered her about the call. She had no idea what it was, but she had an unshakable feeling that something was amiss. She decided to drop by her aging father's apartment and see for herself that he was OK.

When Larry didn't answer the door, Phyllis's faint stirrings of intuition changed to raging alarm bells. She raced for the building manager and had him unlock the door.

It was a heart-breaking sight that awaited her: Larry was sprawled on the bedroom floor. His left wrist was broken under him, where he'd fallen trying to answer the door. He tried to speak, but all that came out was a slurred garble.

Larry was rushed to intensive care, and the doctors concluded that he'd suffered a stroke. The next day, he slipped into a coma, and his chances became so dicey that the doctors stopped speculating on a prognosis. No one was sure if he'd live, and if he did, if he'd ever walk again.

Five days later, Larry came out of the coma and started toiling down the painstaking road to recovery. Half of his body was paralyzed: his left leg and arm were nearly useless. The right side of his face was distorted, and he couldn't speak.

He remained in the hospital for several months, communicating with Phyllis through written notes and receiving the physical therapy that might someday enable him to achieve his new dream: to walk again.

Three months after the stroke, he returned to his apartment in the company of an in-home nurse. A physical therapist visited every day. He had the finest medical care possible, but over the course of the year, he watched his financial resources dwindling.

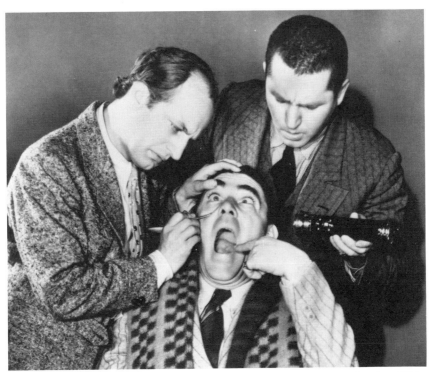

Larry, Moe, and Curly in an early publicity still without the famous hair styles, circa 1934. (from the collection of Jeff & Greg Lenburg)

Phyllis applied for Larry's admittance into the Motion Picture Country House and Hospital in Woodland Hills. This beautiful complex, with its acres of grounds, retirement facilities and hospital is run by the Motion Picture Academy — the same folks who give out the Oscars each year.

It is there that the industry takes care of its own. Any member of a Hollywood Guild or Union, from the lowliest technician to the greatest star, is qualified for admittance to its facilities. If you have funds, you pay. If you're penniless, you cannot be turned away.

It was the perfect solution for Larry. In January, 1971, he was admitted to the Lodge, a section of the facility for patients "on the mend." It had private, furnished rooms, no set visiting hours and a 24-hour nursing staff.

Larry had regained the use of his voice, and we were finally able to talk to him on the phone. It was a little hard to understand him, because his speech was still slurred. But we managed to communicate all right.

"I get to see other people," he'd say. "And I realize that no matter how sick you are, somebody else is worse off than you are. And if you stick to it, you've got to make it. I mean, they gave me up for dead: they said I'd never walk again or talk again. But here I am talking, and I'll be walking. You can bet on that."

FAMILY REUNION ~~~~~~~~~~~~~~ 1973

At the age of 68, I found myself flying in an airplane for the first time in my life. Frankly, I was more than a little apprehensive about the whole thing, but Lyla insisted that it was time for me to visit Larry in California.

"You want he should come visit you?" Lyla would say. "Look, Moe, you're not getting any younger, and neither is Larry."

Lyla was a schoolteacher and had the summer off, so we decided to go together.

The flight went smoothly, thank God. How they get all that heavy metal up in the air, I'll never know. But I could see how people who travel long distances could get used to it. It only took five hours to cross the entire continent. It took longer than that to drive our rental car out to Phyllis's house, get settled, have dinner with Phyllis and her daughter Chris, and finally arrive at Woodland Hills to see Larry.

What a scene that was, when we met him at the Lodge. I hadn't seen Larry for four or five years, and we hugged with joy and cried like babies.

It was a shock, though, to find my brother in a wheelchair. Every doctor in the world could have told me, "Moe, your brother is in a wheelchair," and part of me would still have been disbelieving. I had to see it with my own eyes, and it took some getting used to.

Larry wasn't about to let me brood: he was the hearty host, showing Lyla and me around his sunny, functionally-furnished room. His many sketches and paintings seemed to beam at us from the walls.

Larry's speech was back to normal, and he'd obviously been talking up a storm to make up for lost time. He'd dictated a book-length memoir, *Stroke of Luck,* that was being independently published by long-time Stooge fan James Carone.

The framed testimonial letter from Granada Hills High School, signed by teachers & students, on the wall in Larry's room at the Motion Picture Country Home.

Larry in a Three Stooge's tee shirt.

Larry and other patients in a patriotic recital on July the 4th, Independence Day.
(©Jeff and Greg Lenburg)

About 50 copies sat on his bookshelf, sandwiched between two ceramic watchdogs, Larry Fine originals used as bookends. He gave us each a book, autographed with a flourish.

It was the very first book to chronicle the adventures of the Three Stooges, and while Moe Howard and others were to dispute many of its facts, Larry's voice and wit come through clearly.

"Who's your 'sister Helen'?" Lyla asked him as she looked through the book.

"I changed a few names to protect the innocent," Larry smiled. "I wouldn't want your School Board to see you in a book with the Three Stooges!"

Lyla rolled her eyes: "I think they're on to us anyway, Larry."

"You can show your own movies here," I said, pointing to Larry's 16mm projector.

"Yeah, they have a regular theater here for first-run movies, but I use this when I wanna see the good stuff."

The "good stuff" was his library of Stooge shorts: the Oscar-nominated *Men In Black; The Yolk's On Me,* an obscure 1944 war spoof; the highly-praised *Micro-Phonies,* which served as Ed Bernds's 1945 debut as director; 1952's *Cuckoo On A Choo Choo,* which Larry admired for his Marlon Brando imitation despite the rancor of fans who consider it the worst Stooge film ever made, and Larry's personal favorite, *Scrambled Brains,* a 1951 classic which co-starred Babe London, now a fellow resident of the Motion Picture Home. Theater-owners planning Larry Fine film festivals may consult this list free of charge.

The next day, Larry showed us around the beautifully landscaped grounds. Besides the Lodge where Larry lived, there were dining halls, recreation rooms, an excellent hospital and several cottages for couples.

Everyone there had been in the movie business, and Larry had lots of friends, both old and new, among the residents. We met Jean Hagen, a charming lady who had played Danny Thomas's first wife in the series, *Make Room For Daddy.* After all these years, Larry still cracked up as he introduced me as his "little brother."

Now don't get the idea that Larry was confined to the Motion Picture Home. He could come and go as he pleased. He

One of Larry's many paintings.

Larry, with a painting of an eagle which he gave to Morris.

had his own room at Phyllis's house, and he stayed there with us for the bulk of our visit.

Larry was determined to be as mobile as possible. Even at Phyllis's, he'd occasionally eschew his wheelchair for an upright walker.

It was an important part of his therapy to do what he could unaided. I ached to help him when I saw him struggle to get from his wheelchair to his bed, but he waved me off. He hooked his left leg with his right foot and swung it up on the mattress. It was hard work, but he had the light of battle in his eyes that I hadn't seen since he was fighting to break into show business as a kid.

The signature event of any visit with Larry, in sickness or in health, was a party, and this time, it was a birthday bash for his grandson Eric. The familiar gleams of contentment crept back into Larry's face as Eric walked in with his wife and son, Larry's first great-grandson.

"There's nothing in the world like it, Moe," said Larry. "Nothing like holding your great-grandchild. Think of it: three generations into the future! He could move to Mars if he wanted to!"

While Larry was initiating the latest bud on his family tree to the mysteries of outer space, two old buddies were walking through Phyllis's front door. It was Loretta Haney, of the "Haney Sisters and Fine" act, and her sister, Margueritte.

I felt like the star of *This Is Your Life, Moe Feinberg*. The entire map of the world had changed drastically since I'd seen those "girls" last, and there they were: fit and feisty as ever. We stayed up half the night, yacking about the old days.

By the time Lyla and I had to leave California, we had adjusted ourselves to our brother's new life well enough to sense his daily improvement, his relentless march to recovery.

Larry showed us a letter he'd received from Granada Hills High School. It was hand-written in elegant Old English script, and a lot of time and care had clearly gone into it. But it was the heart-felt words of its author that he was proudest of:

> Dear Larry:
>
> It is difficult to express to you the impact your visit to this High School had on the Student Body. Everyone talks about the "Generation Gap." You closed it.
>
> It has been a long time since anyone received four standing ovations at this school. We really appreciate your time and effort in coming to the first high school in the Valley. Please get well.

THE MIKE DOUGLAS SHOW ⸱⸱⸱⸱⸱⸱⸱⸱ 1974

Larry's illness forced him to limit his personal appearances to the Los Angeles area, but Moe Howard had the entire lecture circuit at his command. He'd answer questions from the audience, provide glimpses into the world of vaudeville, tell jokes and throw pies.

"I never met a face that didn't look better with a pie plastered to it," Moe used to say.

I went to see him tape a Mike Douglas Show at Philadelphia's Channel Three. I hadn't seen Moe or Helen Howard in years, and we had a joyous reunion in the station's green room before the show. Their hair was silver now, but Moe's wisecracks were the same: it was just like the old days backstage at the Earle.

Helen and I retreated to the VIP box, a roped-off square of seats for visiting celebrities, when the show began.

Morris "Moe" Feinberg, 1977.

Moe Howard reliving old times with Mike Douglas as Ted Knight prepares to join in the fun.

Moe Howard with a glint in his eye.

Moe came out with the wiry intensity of a 23-year-old promoting his new movie. Every other line was a laugh-getter.

"Do you have any unfulfilled ambitions?" Mike asked him toward the end of the show.

"Just one," said Moe.

Suddenly, he was charging at the audience with a pie in his hand. Everyone was screaming, but it was the VIP section he was headed for, and I closed my eyes, expecting the worst.

Those of you watching at home saw an anonymous woman take the pie in her face, laughing through the whipped cream.

It was Helen Howard.

"Moe's been rehearsing for that one all his life," she told me after the show. "I'm glad he finally got it out of his system."

IN MEMORIAM 〜〜〜〜〜〜〜 *1975*

Larry had been recovering so nicely that we had hopes that he would join the ranks of Bud Abbott and Bob Hope's stooge, Jerry Colona, fellow stroke victims who had emerged from the Home fit and hale.

But the day before Larry's 72nd birthday, he had another stroke. Even though he bounced back quickly, sounding cheerful on the phone again within two weeks, our hopes had diminished.

He suffered his final stroke on January 9, 1975. He was in a coma for two weeks and died on January 25th.

Larry had been equally at home on both coasts for most of his life, and had left large pockets of loved ones in both Los Angeles and Philadelphia. Phyllis arranged a funeral at Hollywood's Forest Lawn Cemetary where Mabel and Johnny were buried. Lyla's rabbi encouraged us to hold a companion service here in Philadelphia.

We had a beautiful ceremony at her synagogue, but my most powerful memories are of the private *Shiva* that Lyla held afterward.

The *Shiva* is the Jewish ritual of mourning: mirrors are veiled; the mourners make ceremonial tears on their garments. But much of it is life-affirming. When friends and relatives arrive bringing sweets, all talk is in praise of the deceased. Someone will bring hard-boiled eggs, symbolizing the constant renewal of life. Even the *Kaddish,* the Aramaic prayer of mourning, exults in the Lord for creating the wonderful universe.

In that warm spirit, let me tell you Larry's favorite poem, an anonymous verse that invokes Larry's philosophy of clowning:

A PRAYER FOR CLOWNS

God bless all clowns
Who star the world with laughter
Who ring the rafters
With a flying jest.
Who make the world spin merry on its way
And somehow add more beauty to each day.
God bless all clowns
So poor the world would be
Lacking their piquant touch, hilarity.
The belly-laughs, the ringing, lovely mirth
That makes a friendly place of this earth.
God bless all clowns —
Give them a long good life.
Make bright their way — They're a race apart
All comest most who turn their hearts' pain
Into a dazzling jest to lift the heart.
God bless all clowns.

One of the last photos of Larry Fine.
(©Jeff and Greg Lenburg)

Charcoal sketch by Larry.

Larry Fine after his stroke, circa 1973.

Vaude bits were transient things, moments of splendor or hilarity that would unfold before our eyes and vanish into the night air. Most were never published or even written down. Act upon celebrated act passed by the boards, leaving no trail but a handful of reviews and rich memories. We remember a gag or two, a spring in our step as we left the theater, the ambience of magic. The phrasing, the gestures, all the little details are gone.

The Howard, Fine and Howard act was an exception: one of the very few that was actually copied and preserved. We have Mr. J. L. Peterson to thank for that: he was the guy who was hired to produce a written description of the boys' routine as evidence for Healy's lawsuit.

His report shows two skits. The first is an introductory bit in which the boys are brought up onstage to "say hello to the folks" and tell a few jokes. The emcee is the "leader" here, though the boys manage to foil him at every turn. The second skit is a longer, more "formal" act in which the boys are in the foreground, and the emcee is more of a "bit player," a stooge for the stooges.

In the script, the theater's emcee is "M.C." Shemp is "S.H." Larry is "L.F." Moe is "M.H."

And now, without further ado, allow me to present the very first vaude turn by Moe, Larry and Shemp without their mentor. Let the age-old zaniness begin!

M.C.: (to bandleader) They tell me you have some specialty men here this week.

(At mention of specialty men, Howard, Fine and Howard start to rise from orchestra pit, exchange puzzled looks, sit back down, then rise again.)

M.C.: Maybe the folks would like to meet the specialty men.

(Howard, Fine and Howard come up on stage from orchestra pit.)

S.H.: Thank you, folks. Thank you from the bottom of our hearts for this wonderful reception.

M.C.: So these are your specialty men. They don't look like musicians.

S.H.: Well, we are musicians.

M.C.: And, of course, you have heard of John Phillip Sousa.

M.H.: Glad to meet you.

M.C.: Now that you're up here, I want you to say hello to the folks.

All: Hello, folks!

S.H.: (to bandleader) Give us our song now.

(Howard, Fine and Howard sing first 16 bars of *My Future Just Past,* of which only the words, "my future just past," are audible. S.H. sings the words, "my future just went by," instead and is interrupted by M.H.)

M.H.: You're wrong, Ma.

S.H.: I'm right, Aimee.

(S.H. slaps M.H., who slaps S.H. back, who slaps M.H. again, who finally turns and slaps L.H. for no reason. When L.F. puts up no resistance, M.H. pokes him in the eyes to boot.)

M.C.: Now, wait a minute, boys. Let's get together on this thing. What else do you boys do that's good?

S.H.: Hey, if our music chokes you up, wait'll you hear our gags! Get a load of this: I'm walking down the street...

L.F.: O, I know this joke! Then he meets the straight man!

M.C.: The straight man?

L.F.: Yes, the fellow with the rice-bowl haircut!

S.H.: As I was saying before Ignatz broke it up, I walk down the street and I meet the straight man. I recognize him, and he recognizes me. Hello, Moe.

M.H.: Hello, Shemp. Where are you going?

S.H.: I'm going fishing.

M.H.: Have you got worms?

S.H.: Yeah, I got 'em, but I'm going anyway.

(M.H. pulls S.H.'s nose. S.H. slaps M.H.; M.H. pokes L.F.'s eyes. General hubbub and ad lib.)

M.C.: That'll do now, boys. You've said enough, and we can do very nicely without you. So I'll pay you off. (takes out checkbook)

S.H.: What is that? A check?

M.C.: Yes, what about it?

S.H.: Is it good?

M.C.: Why do you ask?

S.H.: Here's what we got last week.

(Howard, Fine and Howard take elastic checks from their pockets and stretch them before the M.C.'s eyes. M.C. pushes all three offstage.)

(M.C. continues with song, but is again interrupted — this time by the whole trio. They try to provide back-up vocals for the M.C., but their harmony is not so good. They leave the stage in a hurry.)

M.C.: It seems that the three ginger kids are anxious to do their stuff. Now, give them a big hand, and maybe the boys will do some thing real nice.

(M.C. milks audience for applause to bring them on again. When they reappear, the orchestra plays eight bars of music, at the end of which the boys raise megaphones to their mouths and produce what is known in slang as a razzberry effect. M.C. admonishes them, and there is a general speaking ad lib.)

212

M.C.: Now, wait a minute. Have you boys got your music with you?

S.H.: Why, sure.

M.C.: Then give it to the boys, and they will play it for you.

(S.H. takes large bundle of music from under arm and throws it over the entire orchestra pit. There is a general speaking ad lib. The band strikes a chord, and the three boys sing:)

All: Jane, Jane,
Just plain Jane,
But I'd rather call you....

(At this point, S.H. stops singing and does a funny tap dance step. He is slapped on the nose for his troubles by M.H. L.F. pushes M.H., who turns about and pokes fingers in his eyes. Finally, M.H. nods head to band leader. Band plays short chord which frightens M.H.)

M.H.: (to M.C.) You know, those guys scare the hell out of me.

(S.H. and M.H. start singing *Jane* again, but L.F. wanders off. M.C. calls M.H.'s attention to the fact that L.F. is not singing:)

M.C.: What's the matter with Moisha?

(M.H. walks over to L.F.)

M.H.: Hey, are you working in this act?

L.F.: Yeah.

M.H.: Well, then, pick it up, or I'll crack your skull open!

(M.H. puts left arm around L.F.'s head, forces it down and brings left hand back up into L.F.'s face, forcing it back. As a finishing touch, he pokes his fingers in L.F.'s eyes. M.H. signals orchestra again to strike a short chord. When they strike the chord, M.H. recoils, but recovers in time to join the boys in singing:)

All: Jane, Jane...

S.H.: I'm doing this against my will.

All: Just plain Jane...

S.H.: I'm not responsible for this.

(M.H. slaps him on the nose and turns to poke L.F. in the eyes.)

S.H.: (to bandleader) Let me have it one more time.

(They give him a very short chord.)

S.H.: To hell with them.

(He ad libs for a moment, then goes into the song:)

S.H.: Jane, Jane,
Just plain Jane...
(He does tap dance again and is slapped on the nose by M. H., who turns around and again pokes finger into L.F.'s eye. L.F. falls to the floor and with his hand makes the sound of horse's hooves. M.H. comes down stage, yelling:

M.H.: Whoa! Whoa! Whoa!

(L.F.'s hoof-beats stop.)

M.H.: Gladys, Gladys! What? Not here? She has deceived me. She promised to meet me at the old bridge at ten o'clock. 'Tis now half past eight, and she is not here yet. How the wind blows!

(L.F. makes noise of wind with mouth.)

213

M.H.: With Gladys as my wife, and those papers in my possession, I can laugh at the world! Curses on that Jack Manly: he stands between me and the woman I love. But she'll be mine yet. How it thunders!

(L.F., then frightened, quickly makes thunder noise with his mouth.)

M.H.: Ah! Someone is coming! How well I know her knock, and how well she knows how to knock!

(At first word, "knock," L.F. stamps his foot to suggest a door knocking.)

M.H.: (to S.H.) Ah! Gladys, my darling!

S.H.: Don't touch me, Carroll Cavanaugh! I have found you out!

(Before M.H. has a chance to reply, L.F. is up on his feet, shouting:)

L.F.: Wait a minute! Hold everything! I demand to see the manager!

(M.H. slaps L.F. twice and pokes his fingers in L.F.'s eyes.)

M.H.: Who's the manager?

L.F.: Okay, you're the manager.

M.H.: (to M.C.) Right here is where we do our guessing contest. We do it, and you guess it.

(M.H. gets into a crouched position. In a distorted shape and tail protruding, he moves about in a grotesque fashion.)

M.C.: I have it. You're looking for a place to sit down.

M.H.: No: it's a midget waltzing.

L.F.: Now, you guess me.

(L.F. moves down stage and stands stationary with a fixed gaze. M.C . watches him closely for awhile.

M.C.: You're meditating.

(L.F. looks behind him, then turns back to the M.C.)

L.F.: I don't think so.

M.C.: Well, I give up.

L.F.: I'm going upstairs.

M.C.: Going upstairs?

L.F.: Yes, I'm on an elevator.

(There is a general ad lib. M.C. shoves L.F. to floor. M.H. picks L.F. up by the hair and pokes fingers in his eyes.)

S.H.: (to M.C.) I'm not in this game. (to bandleader) A little music, please!

(S.H. goes into some sort of a funny dance. While he is dancing, M.H. and L.F. are yelling to the band.)

M.H.: Slower, slower!

L.F.: Faster, faster, faster!

M.H.: Slower!

L.H.: Faster!

(Bandleader, not knowing which tempo to hold, stops the music. M.H. and L.F. go on yelling "Slower!" and "Faster!" for awhile. M.H. turns on L.F., pokes him in the eyes and throws him onto the floor.)

214

M.H.: Let's cut the act and get to the finishing number.

(Orchestra plays *Tears*. M.H. and L.F. sing the song, while S.H. goes into poem about airplanes that have crossed the ocean. He mimes plane taking off and flying.

S.H.: And who made it this time, Mammy? It's your only boy! You'll recognize me when you see the tattoo on my chest!

(M.H. and L.F., thinking he is asking them a question, stop the music.)

M.H.: Who is it?

L.F.: Who is it?

S.H.: Who is it?

L.F.: Is it...

S.H.: Aw, cut it out.

M.H.: (to S.H.) Ahhh! Is that your right face?

S.H.: It ain't anybody else's butt!

(All three boys suddenly realize what S.H. just said and beat a hasty exit with M.C. angrily chasing them off.)

Shemp, Moe, and Larry as "Three Lost Souls."
This is how they looked when they performed the skits above.
(From the collection of Mark Gilman)

215

KEROUAC & THE THREE STOOGES

One of the Three Stooges' most memorable appearances was not on stage, screen or TV, but in the world of literature, as characters in Jack Kerouac's *Visions of Cody*. It was a legendary book—a sprawling apocalypse of the back alleys and open highways of 1950s America, an expanded, unexpurgated telling of the concerns that animated Kerouac's best selling *On The Road*. But for nearly two decades, it existed mainly as a tattered manuscript passed among beatnik literati. Rumors flew that the book marked the invention of a major literary style based on the rhythms of jazz, a "spontaneous bop prosody," as Allen Ginsberg put it, that would revolutionize the novel and just about everything else.

Occasionally, excerpts from the manuscript would emerge from the mists of rumor into public distribution. The first to do so was a piece entitled "Cody and The Three Stooges." It appeared as a reading by the author on a brilliant record produced by Steve Allen for Hanover Records in the late fifties. It was just as brilliant, weird and musical as the gossip had foretold—and twice as funny.

Commercial publishers, though, considered the full manuscript "too experimental," and the book went unpublished until 1972, three years after the author's death.

The character of "Cody"—Cody Pomeray—was modeled after Neal Cassady, the man who also inspired the Dean Moriarty character in Kerouac's *On The Road* and the crazed bus driver of Tom Wolfe's *Electric Kool-Aid Acid Test*. Kerouac himself appears in the book as "Jack Duluoz."

The selection that follows is Kerouac's writing on the Stooges in its entirety. In it, Larry and the boys lead Cody and Jack to an external validation of their inner craziness. If the Three Stooges exist, Kerouac suggests, then the entire universe is nuts, and we should all go out and become beatniks.

CODY & THE THREE STOOGES 〰〰〰〰〰〰
by Jack Kerouac

BUT THE LATEST AND PERHAPS REALLY...best vision, also on high, but under entirely different circumstances, was the vision I had of Cody as he showed me one drowsy afternoon in January, on the sidewalks of workaday San Francisco, just like workaday afternoon on Moody Street in Lowell when boyhood buddy funnyguy G.J. and I played zombie piggy-backs in mill employment offices and workmen's saloons (the Silver Star it was), what and how the Three Stooges are like when they go staggering and knocking each other down the street, Moe Curly (who's actually the bald domed one, big husky) and meaningless goof (though somewhat mysterious as though he was a saint in disguise, a masquerading superduper witch doctor with good intentions actually)—can't think of his name; Cody knows his name, the bushy feathery haired one. Cody was supposed to be looking after his work at the railroad, we had just blasted in the car as we drove down the hill into wild mid-Market traffic and out Third past the Little Harlem where two and a half years ago we jumped with the wild tenor cats and Freddy and the rest...we passed Third Street and all its *that*, and came, driving slowly, noticing everything, talking everything, to the railyards where we worked and got out of the car to cross the warm airy plazas of the day... began somehow talking about the Three Stooges—were headed to see Mrs. So-and-So in the office and on business and around us conductors, executives, commuters, consumers rushed or sometimes just maybe ambling Russian spies carrying bombs in briefcases and sometimes ragbags I bet—just for foolishness—and the station there, the creamy stucco suggestive of palms, like the Union Station in L.A. with its palms and mission arches and marbles, is so unlike a railroad station to an Easterner like myself used to old redbrick and sootirons and exciting gloom fit for snows and voyages across pine forests to the sea, or like that great NYCEP whatever station...that I couldn't imagine anything good and adventurous coming from it...when it came into Cody's head to imitate the stagger of the Stooges, and he did it wild, crazy, yelling in the sidewalk right there by the arches and by hurrying executives, I had a vision of him which at first (manifold it is!) was swamped by the idea that this was one hell of a wild unexpected twist in my suppositions about how he might now in his later years feel, twenty-five, about his employers and their temple and conventions, I saw his (again) rosy flushing face exuding heat and joy, his eyes popping in the hard exercise of staggering, his whole frame of clothes capped by those terrible pants with six, seven holes in them and streaked with baby food, come, ice cream, gasoline, ashes — I saw his whole life, I saw all the movies we'd ever been in, I saw for some reason he and his father on Larimer Street not caring in May — their Sunday afternoon walks hand in hand in back of great baking soda factories and along deadhead tracks and ramps, at the foot of that mighty red brick chimney a la Chirico or Chico Velasquez throwing a huge long shadow across their path in the gravel and the flat —

Supposing the Three Stooges were real? (and so I saw them spring into being at the side of Cody in the street right there in front of the Station, Curly, Moe and Larry, that's his bloody name, *Larry;* Moe the leader, mopish, mowbry, mope-mouthed, mealy, mad, hanking, making the others quake; whacking Curly on the iron pate, backhanding Larry (who wonders); picking up a sledgehammer, honk, and ramming it down nozzle first on the flatpan of Curly's skull, boing, and all big dumb convict Curly does is muckle and yukkle and squeal, pressing his lips, shaking his old butt like jelly, knotting his Jell-o fists, eyeing Moe, who looks back and at him with that lowered and surly "Well what are you gonna do about it?" under thunderstorm eyebrows like the eyebrows of Beethoven, completely ironbound in his surls, Larry in his angelic or rather he really looks like he conned the other two to let him join the group, so they had to pay him all these years a regular share of the salary to them who work so hard with the props — Larry, goofhaired, mopple-lipped, lisped, muxed and completely flunk — trips over a pail of whitewash and falls face first on a seven-inch nail that remains imbedded in his eyebone; the eyebone's connected to the shadowbone, shadowbone's connected to

218

the luck bone, luck bone's connected to the, foul bone, foul bone's connected to the, high bone, high bone's connected to the, air bone, air bone's connected to the, sky bone, sky bone's connected to the, angel bone, angel bone's connected to the, God bone, *God bone's connected to the bone bone;* Moe yanks it out of his eye, impales him with an eight-foot steel rod; it gets worse and worse, it started on an innocent thumbing, which led to backhand, then the pastries, then the nose yanks, blap, bloop, going, going, gong; and now as in a sticky dream set in syrup universe they do muckle and moan and pull and mop about like I told you in an underground hell of their own invention, they are involved and alive, they go haggling down the street at each other's hair, socking, remonstrating, falling, getting up, flailing, as the red sun sails — So supposing the Three Stooges were real and like Cody and me were going to work, only they forget about that, and tragically mistaken and interallied, begin pasting and cuffing each other at the employment office desk as clerks stare; supposing in real gray day and not the gray day of movies and all those afternoons we spent looking at them, in hooky or officially on Sundays among the thousand crackling children of peanuts and candy in the dark show when the Three Stooges (as in that golden dream B-movie of mine round the corner from the Strand) are providing scenes for wild vibrating hysterias as great as the hysterias of hipsters at Jazz at the Philharmonics, supposing in real gray day you saw them coming down Seventh Street looking for jobs — as ushers, insurance salesmen — that way. Then I saw the Three Stooges materialize on the sidewalk, their hair blowing in the wind of things, and Cody was with them, laughing and staggering in savage mimicry of them and himself staggering and gooped but they didn't notice...I followed in back....There was an afternoon when I had found myself hungup in a strange city, maybe after hitch-hiking and escaping something, half tears in my eyes, nineteen or twenty, worrying about my folks and killing time with B-movie or any movie and suddenly the Three Stooges appeared (just the name) goofing on the screen and in the streets that are the same streets as outside the theater only they are photographed in Hollywood by serious crews like Joan Rawshanks in the fog, and the Three Stooges were bopping one another...until, as Cody says, they've been at it for so many years in a thousand climactic efforts super-climbing and worked out every refinement of bopping one another so much that now, if it isn't already over, in the baroque period of the Three Stooges they are finally bopping mechanically and sometimes so hard it's impossible to bear (wince), but by now they've learned not only how to master the style of the blows but the symbol and acceptance of them also, as though inured in their souls and of course long ago in their bodies, to buffetings and crashings in the rixy gloom of Thirties movies and B short subjects (the kind made me yawn at 10 a.m. in my hooky movie of high school days, intent I was on saving my energy for serious-jawed features which in my time was the cleft jaw of Cary Grant), the Stooges don't feel the blows any more, Moe is iron, Curly's dead, Larry's gone, off the rocker, beyond the hell and gone, (so ably hidden by his uncombable mop, in which, as G.J. used to say, he hid a Derringer pistol), so there they are, bonk, boing, and there's Cody following after them stumbling and saying "Hey, lookout, houk" on Larimer or Main Street or Times Square in the mist as they parade erratically like crazy kids past the shoeboxes of simpletons and candy corn arcades — and seriously Cody talking about them, telling me, at the creamy Station, under palms or suggestions thereof, his huge rosy face bent over the time and the thing like a sun, in the great day — So then I knew that long ago when the mist was raw Cody saw the Three Stooges, maybe he just stood outside a pawnshop, or hardware store, or in that perennial poolhall door but maybe more likely on the pavings of the city under tragic rainy telephone poles, and thought of the Three Stooges, suddenly realizing — that life is strange and the Three Stooges exist — that in 10,000 years — that....all the goofs he felt in him were justified in the outside world and he had nothing to reproach himself for, bonk, boing, crash, skittely boom, pow, slam, bang, boom, wham, blam, crack, frap, kerplunk, clatter, clap, blap, fap, slapmap, splat, crunch, crowsh, bong, splat, *BONG!*